New Kinds of Smart

Praise for *New Kinds of Smart*

"I would like to fully endorse this book and compliment the authors on producing a work that is both grounded in solid research and highly relevant to schools seeking effective ways of extending and deepening the achievements of their students. The authors adopt a refreshing and innovative approach which should make this book highly accessible."
Sir William Atkinson, Headteacher, Phoenix High School

"When the only certainty is that the future is uncertain, Bill Lucas and Guy Claxton offer strategic direction to those who aspire to co-nurture learning systems which truly develop talent in all."
Professor Anna Craft, University of Exeter and The Open University

"*New Kinds of Smart* is an intelligent book about intelligence, the many things that go into it, and how educators can help students to get more of the cornucopia.

What intelligence is 'made of' is one of psychology's most contested questions. The authors of *New Kinds of Smart* offer an expansive view grounded in research and carried into the classroom through guidelines and illustrations for deeper practice."
Professor David Perkins, Harvard University, USA

"We need fresh and accessible thinking about learning, in and beyond our education institutions. Bill Lucas and Guy Claxton give us just that – great debate-feeding stuff."
Professor Tom Schuller, author of *Learning Through Life*

"*New Kinds of Smart* is a book for the thinking teacher. . .or the thinking parent, the thinking governor, or the thinking employer. . .anyone who wants to think through some aspects of the education system that we set before our young.

New Kinds of Smart manages the trick of bringing together the story of how schooling approaches have developed, the scientific theories about how people learn and the unfolding reasons for our society's inability to recognise real world learning. Why are some types of learning more valued than others? What is success? How do we know? What do we value in qualifications? Why do many view work with hands less worthy than work in the abstract?

This immensely readable book explains the developments of learning theory and then applies those developments to classroom practice and takes that next vital step of explaining what that means for a learner. This is followed by well grounded advice on how to use all this insight to help people to learn better. . .the ultimate role of the teacher.

New Kinds of Smart is one of those books that can be read in one sitting or just as much enjoyed by dipping in; it is full of nuggets. Enjoy it. . .and use it well."
Professor Mick Waters, Chairman of The Curriculum Foundation

"This is an important and welcome book. It cuts through the hype about what the latest findings from cognitive neuroscience can, and more important, cannot tell us, and provides a comprehensive overview of what we know about learning. This is not a 'how to' book – because teaching is far too complex to be reduced to a set of instructions – but it does suggest practical steps that teachers can take in designing more effective learning experiences for their students. For parents, it provides a clear vision of what learning could be like – and indeed will have to be like if we are to prepare young people to thrive in a world we cannot possibly imagine. If your child's school is not offering what is envisaged here, ask why not?"
Professor Dylan Wiliam, Institute of Education, University of London

New Kinds of Smart

How the science of learnable intelligence is changing education

Bill Lucas and Guy Claxton

Open University Press

Open University Press
McGraw-Hill Education
McGraw-Hill House
Shoppenhangers Road
Maidenhead
Berkshire
England
SL6 2QL

email: enquiries@openup.co.uk
world wide web: www.openup.co.uk

and Two Penn Plaza, New York, NY 10121-2289, USA

First published 2010
Reprinted 2011

Copyright © Bill Lucas and Guy Claxton 2010

A catalogue record of this book is available from the British Library

ISBN13: 978-0-33-523618-3 (pb)   978-0-33-523619-0 (hb)
ISBN10: 0-33-523618-9 (pb)   0-33-523619-7 (hb)

Library of Congress Cataloging-in-Publication Data
CIP data applied for

Typeset by RefineCatch Limited, Bungay, Suffolk
Printed in the UK by Bell and Bain Ltd, Glasgow.

Fictitious names of companies, products, people, characters and/or data that
may be used herein (in case studies or in examples) are not intended to
represent any real individual, company, product or event.

The McGraw·Hill Companies

Mixed Sources
Product group from well-managed
forests and other controlled sources
www.fsc.org   Cert no. TT-COC-002769
© 1996 Forest Stewardship Council

FSC

Contents

CONTENTS

CONTENTS

Series Editors' Introduction

In confronting the many challenges that the future holds in store, humankind sees in education an indispensable asset . . .

Jaques Delors et al[1]

The dizzying speed of the modern world puts education at the heart of both personal and community development; its mission is to enable everyone, without exception, to develop all their talents to the full and to realize their creative potential, including responsibility for their own lives and achievement of their personal aims.

Education, unfortunately, doesn't always keep up with the times. Sometimes it appears to be moving in step with changes; at other times it still seems to be in the past century. Many years of research have shown us that tinkering around the edges of schooling won't help educators meet the challenges that children and young people will face in their future. Current interventions are having limited effects.[2] Even if levels of attainment are getting better, the gap in educational achievement between the most and least advantaged is far too wide in many places. Every child and young person has to be well equipped to seize learning opportunities throughout life, to broaden her or his knowledge, skills and attitudes, and to be able to adapt to a changing, complex and interconnected world. It's possible to maximize the opportunity of achieving 'preferred futures'[3] for children and young people, for the teaching profession, and for schools. But what's required is a bold and imaginative reorientation to educational purposes, policies and practices.

In this series, we want to provide a forum for suggesting and thinking about different and more powerful ways of ensuring that all students are prepared to take an active and proactive role in their future, that all teachers and other adults are best able to help them learn effectively, that all leaders and community members can rise to the challenges of ensuring that nothing stands in their way, and that learning environments are designed in such a way to ensure this high level learning and success for all students. We believe it's time to expand educational horizons.

Authors in this international series provide fresh views on things we take for granted and alternative ways of addressing educational challenges. Exploring trends, ideas, current and emerging developments and professional learning needs, they offer a variety of perspectives of what education could be; not what it has been or, even, is. The books are designed to engage your imagination, to inform, to encourage you to 'look beyond' and help others to do so, to challenge thinking, to inspire, to motivate, to promote deep reflection, collaboration and thoughtful action, to stimulate learning and deep change; and to offer avenues of action and concrete possibilities.

We hope that the series will appeal to a wide audience of practitioners, local authority/district personnel, professional developers, policy makers and applied academics working in a variety of different contexts and countries. Primarily, we are looking to support and challenge busy professionals working in education who don't always feel they have time to read books. The research on professional learning that makes a difference is clear: educators need the stimulus of external ideas.[4] The books are intended for use by people in schools/centres/colleges, local authorities/districts, consultants; national, state and regional policy makers; and professional developers for example, those involved in leadership development. They will be valuable for people involved in ongoing professional learning programmes. They may also be important additions to Masters courses that are geared to investigating practice as it is and as it might be.

The books are deliberately relatively short, laid out in a way that we hope will add to readability, and contain practical suggestions for action, questions for reflection and to stimulate learning conversations, highlighted quotes and suggested follow-up readings. Each book can be read as a stand alone, but the focus on looking beyond what is to what might be is the linking feature, and each book has a broadly similar format, to facilitate the connections.

In this thoughtful and uplifting book, *New Kinds of Smart: How the Science of Learnable Intelligence is Changing Education,* Bill Lucas and Guy Claxton push us to think more radically about what it means to be intelligent in a fast changing world. New discoveries have emerged from the learning sciences that the educational world simply hasn't taken on board. Drawing on compelling research, they challenge fondly held and enduring myths about the nature of intelligence, offering practical examples and pointers for action. They make no claims that they have all the answers – like the learning sciences, it is a 'work in progress' – but they invite the reader to join them on a journey of continuing discovery. It's a journey well worth taking.

Louise Stoll and Lorna Earl

References

1 Delors, J., Al Mufti, I., Amagi, A., et al. (1996) *Learning: The Treasure Within – Report to UNESCO of the International Commission on Education for the Twenty-first Century.* Paris: UNESCO.
2 Stein, M.K., and Coburn, C.E. (2003) Toward producing usable knowledge for the improvement of educational practice: a conceptual framework. In Abstracts, Biennial Meeting of the European Conference for Research on Learning and Instruction. Padova, Italy.

   Elmore, R. (2004) *School Reform from the Inside Out: Policy, Practice and Performance.* Cambridge: Harvard Education Press.
3 Beare, H. (2001). *Creating the Future School.* London: RoutledgeFalmer.
4 Cordingley, P., Bell, M., Isham, C., Evans, D. Firth, A. (2007) What do specialists do in CPD programmes for which there is evidence of positive outcomes for pupils and teachers? Report. In: *Research Evidence in Education Library.* London: EPPI-Centre, Social Science Research Unit, Institute of Education, University of London.

   Timperley, H., Wilson, A., Barrar, H. and Fung, I. (2008) *Teacher Professional Learning and Development: Best Evidence Synthesis Iteration.* New Zealand Ministry of Education.

Acknowledgements

This book had its seeds in earlier discussions under the aegis of The Talent Foundation and we would like particularly to thank Sebastian Bailey (and The Mind Gym), Sir Christopher Ball, Andy Powell (and the Edge Foundation), Toby Greany, Eugene Sadler-Smith and Louise Stoll (who gets a special extra thanks for being one of our editors on this book, too!). We have also benefited from the vast expertise of our friends at TLO Ltd, especially Maryl Chambers and Graham Powell, and from stimulating discussions with Margaret Carr, Peter Davies, Howard Gardner, Ellen Langer, David Perkins, William Richardson, Jonathan Rowson, Richard Sennett, and Chris Watkins.

We are most grateful to Lorna Earl, Fiona Richman and all of the team at Open University Press for their helpful and supportive comments.

Our special thanks go to Jenny Elmer and Rob Webster at the Centre for Real-World Learning for their detailed reading of earlier drafts and for their many specific suggestions for improving the book.

And of course to our patient, supportive partners, Henrietta Lucas and Judith Nesbitt.

About the authors

Bill Lucas is Co-Director of the Centre for Real-World Learning and Professor of Learning at the University of Winchester. While CEO of the UK's Campaign for Learning he set up the first ever national research project into learning to learn in schools in England. He is the author of many books including *The Creative Thinking Plan* (with Guy) (BBC Books, 2007); *Happy Families: How to Make One, How to Keep One* (BBC Active, 2006); and *Power Up Your Mind: Learn Faster, Work Smarter* (Nicholas Brealey Publishing, 2002).

Guy Claxton is Co-Director of the Centre for Real-World Learning and Professor of the Learning Sciences at the University of Winchester. Guy is the originator of the 'Building Learning Power' programme now widely used in schools across the world. His many books include: *What's the Point of School? Rediscovering the Heart of Education* (Oneworld, 2008); *Building Learning Power: Helping Young People Become Better Learners* (TLO, 2002), and *Hare Brain, Tortoise Mind: Why Intelligence Increases When You Think Less* (Fourth Estate, 1997).

About the Centre for Real-World Learning (CRL)

CRL's aim is to understand better the kinds of intelligence that enable people to pursue real-life interests and respond to real-life challenges. Through research and knowledge-exchange activities, CRL helps people to get better at getting better at the things that really matter to them. CRL is specifically interested in exploring the way that the learning sciences can be better understood and applied in education, and how school can be a more effective preparation for a lifetime of learning.

Prelude

The goal of early education (and perhaps of all education)
should not be seen as simply that of training brains whose
basic potential is already determined. Rather, the goal is to
provide rich environments in which to grow better brains.

Andy Clark[1]

A short while ago we worked with the UK's Talent Foundation[2] to identify and analyse a large amount of new thinking about intelligence from many different disciplines. The collaboration was enough to convince us that the learning sciences are developing apace and that the educational world simply has not caught up with some of this emerging thinking. The present book was born from this review and its ideas have been further fuelled by interactions with many academic and practitioner colleagues, as well as through our own enquiries over a number of years.

New Kinds of Smart: How the Science of Learnable Intelligence Is Changing Education is written for enquiring practitioners. We imagine it being read by teachers and educational leaders (whoever

NEW KINDS OF SMART

and wherever they may be). These are the kind of people who may well already be investigating the new kinds of thinking we explore in the book and who are determined to bring more scientific approaches to the craft of teaching. We hope *New Kinds of Smart* may also strike a chord with anyone training tomorrow's teachers and classroom assistants. Teachers reading this who are parents may well see implications for their parenting, too.

Format of the book

The book works like this. It has eight core chapters, each of which follows a similar format:

A specific piece of research which illustrates the theme of the chapter.

⇩

Getting to grips with. An overview of scientific and educational research relevant to the chapter.

⇩

Starting out. Examples of what schools that are just beginning to work with the ideas in the chapter are doing.

⇩

> *Going deeper.* More advanced examples of the ways in which schools are working with the ideas in the chapter.

⇩

> *Ideas into practice.* Questions to prompt thinking, reflection, discussion, action and further reading.

At an appropriate moment in each chapter we have also included a useful tool to enable you immediately to see how you could move from thinking into action.

While Chapters 7 and 8 follow the same format as the previous six, they are somehow larger in scope. Chapter 7 deals with the way people can organize and orchestrate the resources they have at their disposal more strategically, so that they maximize their overall smartness. Chapter 8 looks at intelligence operating in the wider world, and comes back to the fundamental – moral – question of what intelligence is for. We argue that you cannot properly understand intelligence without attending to the bigger ethical responsibilities at play.

Bracketing these central eight chapters are two different kind of chapters. The *Prelude* – the chapter you are reading now – sets the scene and anticipates the content of the book. It also exposes some prevailing myths and assumptions about intelligence and argues for a different approach to teaching and learning.

And at the end there is a *Finale* to round off the book. Here we summarize where we think we have got to, and look ahead, sharing some of the work of the Centre for Real-World Learning at the University of Winchester[3] with regard both to schools and the wider educational context of lifelong learning. In particular, we will review the steps we have made, towards a richer and more valid model of 'real-world intelligence'.

The musical connection implied by our choice of *Prelude* and *Finale* is not accidental. For there is an underlying metaphor, which runs throughout the book, of intelligence requiring us to 'play together', like the instruments that go to make up an orchestra. The different aspects of intelligence described in the central chapters of the book, certainly in the first six, represent different kinds of instruments. Only when they are all playing together in time and in tune can the symphony emerge in all its glory. At such moments you are truly exploiting the full scope of what it is to be smart today. Chapter 7 – 'Intelligence is Strategic' – reminds us of the role of the intelligent orchestra's 'conductor'. Chapter 8 suggests that, while one orchestra may sound tuneful, we need to live on a planet in which lots of orchestras can flourish for many years to come; we need, in short to bring an ethical dimension to the important role of 'growing better brains'.

In the rest of this Prelude, we will briefly introduce some of the major themes that the rest of the book is going to explore in more detail. So without more ado let's ask: 'what's the "score" that we will be following?'

What's the point of school?[4]

Education is a preparation for life, and the nature of that preparation depends on a number of assumptions and perceptions. What schools are set up to do depends on society's view of the world –

especially the world which it imagines its young people will inhabit when they are grown up – and on the difficulties, challenges and opportunities which it thinks that world will present. Those challenges are to do with national prosperity and security; social cohesion and equity; and individual fulfilment and well-being.

From such complex sets of assumptions each nation has to take a view of what it is that all young people need to know, understand, and be able to do, if they are to meet those challenges, and take advantage of those opportunities, as well as they can. For example, many people today think that, above all, we are preparing children and young people for a world of change. Paradoxically, such people agree that the only thing that people can say with any certainty about the challenges which lie ahead is that they do not know exactly what they will be – so deciding what and how to teach is a problem. We agree.

But the curriculum also depends on assumptions about young people and their families. Much of what young people will need – the ability to walk, feed themselves, and learn to speak their mother tongue, for example – are assumed to happen just in the normal process of growing up. Families lay many of the foundations for life. But there are other areas of supposedly essential development where society judges that family life cannot be guaranteed to provide what is needed – or not reliably enough for all young people.

In such cases, schools step in to provide the bits of that vital preparation that might not otherwise happen. For example, if families cannot be relied upon to cultivate the abilities to read, write and calculate, to the levels that society thinks is necessary, then young people should go to places that will ensure that the requisite learning comes about. And so on. The design of an education system has to reflect many assumptions – about the future, about what 'fulfilment' means, about family life – many of which are contested. No wonder education is so contentious.

Changing views of developing young minds

But there is another set of assumptions on which education rests that is not to do with society, but to do with the nature and capacities of children's minds. How do their minds mature? What 'ought' they to be capable of doing and learning at different ages? What is 'normal' for a 5-year-old, and how much can children vary from that norm before we start to get worried about them, and think about giving them special provision to help them 'catch up'? What useful learning can their minds acquire, as it were, by osmosis from the process of life itself, and what has to be specially orchestrated or stimulated? How much does their experience change not only *what* they think and know, but the way they go about thinking and knowing?

We do not generally assume that we have to lay on special classes in 'seeing', but many people think that children do need specialized help in learning to 'think', for example. Yet people differ markedly in their beliefs about how much of the difference between children – in, say, how well they think and learn and remember – reflects factors over which a teacher can have no control, such as their genetic make-up or earliest experiences, and how much is capable of being systematically trained and developed. Can young people learn to be better rememberers, or better at concentrating, or better at meeting new challenges? Are some children just born 'bright', and therefore destined – no matter how much we try to help

– to learn faster and deeper than others born 'average' or 'weak'? Or are those differences capable of being moderated by school? Is school a place where you can 'get smarter'? The answers to these questions, too, will exert a powerful influence on what a curriculum is designed to do: what it is assumed to be capable, or not capable, of doing.

As each of these sets of assumptions changes, or comes under scrutiny, so the enterprise of education is liable to change. If we assume that schooling today is largely satisfactory, and that tomorrow – the world we are educating youngsters to cope with – is going to be much like today, then we might be inclined to adopt a 'steady as she goes' approach, with a bit of tinkering and adjustment here and there to nudge up the literacy and examination scores. The knowledge that served *us* well in the past ought to serve *them* well in the future. And the division of the school system into a strand that prepared some young people for university, the professions and 'leadership', and another that prepared people for a rather different kind of life, could seem somehow inevitable and fitting.

But if we see the world as fast-changing, and as demanding of young people a different set of skills and attitudes if they are to thrive and prosper, then we will see the world of education as needing to change in far more radical and urgent ways. Today, most govern-ments around the world, and most teachers, tend to the latter rather than the former view – and so do we.[5]

But the desire for change, and the directions in which it will be sought, will be limited or thwarted if old and unjustified assump-tions about the nature of children's minds – indeed, about the nature of learning itself – are left in place, unexamined. If we were to carry on assuming that some children are born 'intelligent', while others simply do not have the 'brain-power' required to master difficult

> **"**If we were to carry on assuming that some children are born 'intelligent', while others simply do not have the 'brain-power' required to master difficult ideas in physics or history, say, then the options for change, however pressing that change is felt to be, will be limited. If, on the other hand, intelligence is seen as itself learnable, then a whole different set of educational possibilities become thinkable.**"**

ideas in physics or history, say, then the options for change, however pressing that change is felt to be, will be limited. If, on the other hand, intelligence is seen as itself learnable, then a whole different set of educational possibilities become thinkable.

It is no coincidence that, at the same time as the social functions of education are being re-examined, its psychological foundations are also under scrutiny. The very nature of 'intelligence' itself is undergoing a radical reappraisal, and many people are questioning whether the assumptions about children's minds which have underpinned education for a long time are as valid as we have thought. It is on these beliefs about the power and potential of children's minds, and especially the nature of their 'intelligence', that this book focuses.

Challenging some myths about intelligence

It seems to us that the education system is the victim of a number of enduring myths with regard to intelligence and that these are at best unhelpful and at worst downright harmful. Here are some of the beliefs that we will be seeking to challenge in the book. Each one of these broadly speaking relates to the chapter number next to it. Of course such connections are more complex than this so the linear link is not always quite so clear-cut.

Eight myths about intelligence

1 MYTH: Intelligence is essentially a one-dimensional commodity largely to be found in the kinds of thinking required by IQ tests.

2 MYTH: Intelligence is relatively fixed: educators make use of it, but do not really alter it.

3 MYTH: Mind and body are separate and truly intelligent activity is located in the mind.

4 MYTH: Intelligence is rational and conscious.

5 MYTH: Intelligence is a personal 'possession', and using tools which have the effect of making you smarter is a kind of cheating.

6 MYTH: Intelligence is an individual not a social concept.

7 MYTH: The concept of intelligence is universally valid, and not closely tied to the details and demands of one's particular 'habitat'.

8 MYTH: Intelligence is an intellectual function, separate from emotional and moral functions.

If teachers believe some or all of these ideas, then the possibilities of their job are rather constrained. If you are persuaded by the arguments in this book, however, then the job of the educator, whether in school, at home, or in the wider community, becomes a very different one. A range of different possibilities open up. While you (assuming you are an educator of some kind) will still need to locate

> "As well as teaching the 'content' or 'subject' you may now be on the look-out for specific learning strategies designed to boost the learner's mind power."

your learning and teaching activity within real contexts – you cannot develop intelligence or 'grow' better learners in the abstract – you may well come to see your teaching differently. For as well as teaching the 'content' or 'subject' you may now be on the look-out for specific learning strategies designed to boost the learner's mind power.

As with the myths listed above, each of the suggestions below for the development of the teacher's role is deliberately tied to the chapter number next to it. The list, therefore, offers some headline messages from each chapter on what the role of today's teachers might be. If these headlines seem a little cryptic right now, the chapters that follow will spell them out in practical detail. We have put the key concepts in italics.

Eight aspects of the teacher's role in developing more intelligent learners

1. Cultivating the *dispositions* which are most likely to create learners who are active throughout their lives.

2. Developing and sustaining *growth mindsets* in young people (and modelling these as adult learners).

3. Creating opportunities for young people to become more *'manipulate'* as well as articulate.

4. Helping students to develop *states of mind* conducive to different kinds of learning, specifically using their intuitive as well as rational selves.

5　Encouraging learners to understand which *tools* tend to help in certain situations and how to know when to use these.

6　Providing students with effective strategies for learning and working *collaboratively*.

7　Teaching students how to be more *strategic* about their learning, how to reflect on what happens and how to *transfer* their learning from one domain to another.

8　Setting all educational work in a broader *ethical* context in which the ultimate intelligence is the survival of *Homo sapiens* in a fast-changing world.

While each of the chapters in the book follows the format outlined on pages 2–3, some are more richly developed than others. The reason for this is simple. Some areas of the emerging science have caught on quickly in education; others are still under development, and their educational implications are not yet as well worked out. So, for example, sometimes there is the beginning of a practitioner movement (as when seeking to understand strategic intelligence and the ways in which teachers can help students to get better at learning how to learn). Whereas with practical intelligence, where thinking about embodied cognition has not yet found its way into many classrooms, the examples are less developed. But we have nevertheless tried to make some suggestions and point the way.

We hope, whatever your role in education, that you will find the ideas in this book both challenging and useful. This new thinking about intelligence is 'work in progress' and we hope you may be inspired to help that work become both more rigorous and more practical.

1

Intelligence is Composite

Intelligence is a complex mixture of ingredients.

Robert Sternberg[1]

Intelligence is the habit of persistently trying to understand things and make them function better. Intelligence is working to figure things out, varying strategies until a workable solution is found . . . One's intelligence is the sum of one's habits of mind.

Lauren Resnick[2]

Give a group of 13-year-olds an IQ test, and then look at their school grades. You will find that students with the same IQ score differ markedly on how well they are doing in school. Angela Duckworth and Martin Seligman at the University of Pennsylvania wanted to find out why.[3] So they tested the same students on a range of other measures to do with their self-discipline and self-control. They were given a quiz that measured how impulsive they were. They were given a test that asked them to choose between getting a small reward immediately or a larger one after a delay. And their parents and teachers were asked to rate them on how much self-control they thought each student had.

The performance of the more self-disciplined students differed from their equally 'intelligent' but more impulsive counterparts in a number of ways. They were getting better test scores. They were absent less from school. And they spent more time on their homework and less time watching television. Overall, the level of their self-discipline was more than twice as effective as their IQ in accounting for their school performance. More than this, self-discipline predicted which students would improve their grades over the course of the ensuing school year, while IQ did not.

When it comes to getting significant things done in the real world – whether it is doing as well as you can at school or becoming a better goal-kicker – there is clearly a good deal more at stake than IQ. Being smart in real life involves a whole variety of abilities. Even if intelligence were some kind of abstract quality inside your head that was separate from everything else, in practice, as soon as you start to do anything at all complicated or worthwhile, many of these other factors come into play. Being good at the kind of abstract reasoning required by IQ tests may contribute to real-life projects, but its contribution often turns out to be quite small, compared with a host of other personal skills and attitudes. In Duckworth and Seligman's study, IQ was shown to be much less important than the ability to prioritize long-term goals over short-term enjoyment. But self-control is just one of these myriad of other factors.

> ❝Being good at the kind of abstract reasoning required by IQ tests may contribute to real-life projects, but its contribution often turns out to be quite small, compared with a host of other personal skills and attitudes.❞

13

In this chapter, we are going to take intelligence to bits, and take a look at some of the many components of which it might be made up. But, first, let's take a quick look at the history of this issue: the question of whether intelligence is the mind's single most powerful instrument, or whether it is actually an orchestra, made up of many different sections and instruments playing together.

Getting to grips with composite intelligence

Alfred Binet, the father of the IQ test, is often thought of as the villain of this particular piece; but that reputation is unjustified. Although he was indeed involved in the development of the IQ test, he did not think that intelligence was a fixed commodity, and he certainly did not think it was a simple, unitary idea distinct from other human faculties such as perception and personality. On the contrary, he saw intelligence as a complicated mixture of a great many different skills and abilities, and thought that, if intelligence was to be tested, it ought to be sought in as many different kinds of tasks as possible. He thought this variety was so important that he made it a point of principle, writing: 'One might almost say it matters very little what the tests are so long as they are numerous.'[4] Binet's own composite intelligence test included distinguishing pretty from ugly faces (!), executing three commands given simultaneously, naming the months of the year in order, and finding three rhymes for a given word in less than a minute.

The tendency to think of intelligence as a single, unitary quality gained strength from three directions: history, language and measurement. From history came the idea that intelligence is some-how higher than, and different from, other human qualities such as perception or empathy. When Descartes was trying to find the indisputable essence of his humanness, he thought he had found it in his ability to think rationally. Reason enabled him to escape from the untrustworthiness of feeling and experience, and find something lasting and incorruptible in his ability to think logically and system- atically *about anything*. It was clear to him that such reasoning could not be the product of mere matter (even the brain) and had to reflect the God-given rationality that set men (*sic*) apart from children and animals, and, by implication, women.

The very word 'intelligence' invites us to imagine there is a single (albeit mysterious) faculty that underlies intelligent behaviour. When we turn things from adjectives – 'intelligent' – into abstract nouns – 'intelligence' – it is as if we were naming a kind of powerful cause that lies behind the act itself. Why is he able to act intelli- gently? Because he 'possesses intelligence'. And how do you know that he possesses intelligence? Well, obviously, because he acted intelligently. This kind of circular thinking can stop us looking for more complicated and differentiated *sets* of causes.

Similarly, the invention of IQ as a single measure of 'intelli- gence' seems to suggest that there is a single quantity that the test is measuring. But there is no logical reason why we should make this jump in our thinking about intelligence. After all, we know that the single measure 'blood pressure' is a reflection of a large number of intricate interactions going on in the body behind the scenes. It is just as likely that the apparent existence of a single faculty of intelligence reflects the fact that many of the tasks on which IQ is based recruit similar, overlapping sets of more elementary cognitive tools and abilities. As Harvard professor David Perkins has con- cluded, 'The *g* factor [the supposedly unitary source of general intelligence] represents not a single central intellectual ability, but

> **"**Just as a musical group's performance reflects the complex working-together of a whole variety of different instruments, so it appears that the mind creates the appearance of seamless intelligence from the interaction of a whole range of different mental and emotional components.**"**

rather the average overlap in the [collection of] abilities demanded by one task and another.'[5]

Just as a musical group's performance reflects the complex working-together of a whole variety of different instruments, so it appears that the mind creates the appearance of seamless intelligence from the interaction of a whole range of different mental and emotional components. In recent years, there have been many attempts to rescue the idea of intelligence from the monolithic assumption. Let's look at a small sample of these attempts to describe intelligence as an orchestra.

Multiple intelligences

One of the best-known approaches is Howard Gardner's theory of 'multiple intelligences' (MI). On the basis of research on the brain, and especially brain injuries, Gardner identified originally seven, now eight, distinct 'biopsychological potentials', as he called them, that everyone has in differing degrees. The MIs achieved a great deal of popularity with teachers, not least because they seem to map quite neatly onto the core subjects of the traditional school curriculum. *Linguistic intelligence* and *logical-mathematical intelligence* coincide happily with English (and Modern Foreign Languages) and Maths. There is *musical intelligence*, but interestingly no 'aesthetic intelligence' to map onto Art. *Bodily-kinaesthetic intelligence* is the province of Physical Education, Sport and Dance,

Spatial intelligence applied to the Geography of the great explorers, and to the practical sensibility of Design and Technology. The last two of the original seven were called *interpersonal intelligence* – the ability to understand other people – and *intrapersonal intelligence*, the capacity for self-knowledge and self-regulation. These could be found in schools in Personal, Social and Health Education, or what used to be called 'pastoral care'.

Gardner has subsequently discussed what he considers to be three other strong candidates for 'intelligence-hood' – *naturalist intelligence*, *spiritual intelligence* and *existential intelligence* – though on further consideration he decided to combine the latter two into one, admitting only naturalist intelligence into the enlarged group of eight MIs. One of the reasons that Gardner's approach has been contested is the apparent ease with which new intelligences can, like new words, be coined. (It would be tempting to speculate that *cyberworld intelligence* and *financial intelligence* might be in the pipeline!)

Not only did MI theory seem to fit comfortably with the school curriculum, it freed teachers from the need to place all children along a single scale of intelligence. The traditional Cartesian notion of abstract, rational intelligence is associated with only two out of Gardner's eight MIs – a conflation of linguistic and logical-mathematical intelligences. By expanding the list, teachers were usefully given permission, as it were, to value alternative talents and abilities in their students. If being good at the piano or football was not just a skill but an 'intelligence', budding instrumentalists and sportsmen and women could be more highly esteemed, and, for many teachers, that is very important. It also legitimated the role of teacher as coach or talent scout rather than instructor or assessor.

Though the impulse to break the idea of intelligence down into its components is surely right, not everyone agrees that the MI framework is the best way to do it. As we will see in a moment, others have divided intelligence in quite different ways. Howard Gardner himself has been driven to repudiate some of the things that have been done, in some schools, in the name of multiple intelligences. In *Intelligence Reframed*, for example, he wrote:

> I once watched a series of videos about multiple intelligences in the schools. In one video after another I saw youngsters crawling across the floor with the superimposed legend 'Bodily-Kinesthetic Intelligence'. I said, 'That is not bodily-kinesthetic intelligence; that is kids crawling across the floor. And I feel like crawling up the wall.'[6]

Gardner presents MI as a fully-fledged scientific theory and is robustly self-analytical when others challenge his evidence. So some researchers, for example, have questioned the basis on which he has identified his intelligences.[7] And Gardner himself says that at one point that 'it must be admitted that the selection (or rejection) of a candidate intelligence is reminiscent more of an artistic judgment than of a scientific assessment'.[8]

From our point of view, though, while we recognize the fruitful role Gardner has had in broadening the scope of the discussion about intelligence, he does not make it very clear whether each of the eight intelligences is itself learnable. Can you expand your 'naturalistic intelligence', or do you just make the best use of the fixed amount you were given? We'll see in the next chapter that many people are now homing in on the idea of learnable intelligence, so it may be that MI theory gets us only part way towards a better conception of real-world intelligence.

Analytical, creative and practical intelligence

Where Gardner's typology stays close to distinct domains of human activity – mathematics, music, and so on – other people have carved up intelligence in different ways. Robert Sternberg writes about *successful intelligence*,[9] which he considers to be a composite of *academic or analytical intelligence, creative intelligence* and *practical intelligence*. Analytical intelligence refers to the ability to solve problems using good-quality thinking; creative intelligence refers to the antecedent ability to discover or select good problems to work on, and to generate good ideas that the process of thinking can get to work on. Practical intelligence is the ability to actually get things done and make them work in the real world.

Sternberg has shown, in a range of experiments, that these three intelligences can be measured; and that much of conventional education discriminates against people who may be very bright, creatively and practically, but who don't shine analytically or academically. He says: 'Students with creative and practical abilities are essentially "iced out" of the system, because at no point are they much allowed to let their abilities shine through and help them perform better in school.'[10]

> "Students with creative and practical abilities are essentially 'iced out' of the system, because at no point are they much allowed to let their abilities shine through and help them perform better in school."
>
> Robert Sternberg

More than Gardner, Sternberg presents his three kinds of intelligence as capable of expansion (see the next chapter for more on this). But he does not have much to say about how to go about expanding them. And perhaps one of the reasons for this is that the 'grain' of his analysis is too coarse. After all, creativity is not a single faculty, any more than intelligence is. To be creative takes a host of strategies and attitudes, all interwoven in the right way. So ideas like 'creative intelligence', though an improvement, may still be too big to get a practical handle on. We may need to go to a higher level of magnification, so to speak, and look at what goes to make up intelligence in greater detail.

Moving towards learning dispositions

Art Costa and Bena Kallick have done just that. They have broken intelligence down into what they call the *16 habits of mind*.[11] You could look at the habits of mind as a finer-grain specification of what Sternberg meant by analytical, creative and practical intelligence. Instead of just talking about the 'woodwind section' in the mental orchestra, Costa and Kallick begin to distinguish the oboes from the flutes. These are their ingredients of the intelligent mind:

1 *Persisting.* Sticking to a task; seeing things through; staying focused.

2 *Managing impulsivity.* Not rushing into things; taking your time; staying calm, thoughtful and deliberate.

3 *Listening with understanding and empathy.* Seeking to understand others; being able to put your own ideas and opinions 'on hold' in order to see how things look from other people's points of view.

4 *Thinking flexibly.* Being able to come at tricky situations in

different ways; being able to change perspective and consider options.

5 *Thinking about thinking (metacognition).* Being able to stand back from your own thoughts and be aware of them; being strategic about your own thinking.

6 *Striving for accuracy.* Doing your best to 'get it right'; checking answers.

7 *Questioning and posing problems.* Being curious and finding interesting problems to solve.

8 *Applying past knowledge to new situations.* Mobilizing what you already know to help you learn; looking for opportunities to transfer skills to new situations.

9 *Thinking and communicating with clarity and precision.* Trying to avoid over-generalizations and vagueness in both speech and writing.

10 *Gathering data through all the senses.* Being open to information from a wide variety of sources, and in a wide variety of forms.

11 *Creating, imagining, innovating.* Using imagination to generate novel ideas and possibilities.

12 *Responding with wonderment and awe.* Allowing yourself to be intrigued by things; appreciating the mystery and beauty of the world.

13 *Taking responsible risks.* Daring to live on the edge of your competence; being willing to 'give it a go'.

14 *Finding humour.* Looking for things that are whimsical, comical or incongruous in life; being able to laugh at yourself.

15 *Thinking interdependently.* Being able to work and learn well with other people; learning from others.

16 *Remaining open to continuous learning.* Being open to new experiences; being willing to admit ignorance and mistakes.

You'll see that Costa and Kallick have carved up intelligence in quite a different way from MI theory. Their aim is to get below the surface of the mind and identify more of the different psychological instruments that go to make up the orchestra of intelligence. Their claim is that collectively these habits of mind map the different sections of the orchestra quite well. As in the playing of a real symphony orchestra, there may be passages where only one instrument is playing solo: you may just be lost in a state of awe and wonder (Habit no. 12) without doing anything else about it. But then other instruments may join in, as you start using your imagination (no. 11) to try to figure out possible explanations; and then you decide to go online and see what information you can find (no. 10); and you start searching your memory for other things you might already know (no. 8); and then you might say to yourself, 'Hold on a minute, what am I missing here?' (no. 5); and before you know it the whole orchestra has joined in and is playing a complicated set of harmonies and melodies all together.

Costa and Kallick's aim – like our aim in this book – is not just to explain what the orchestra of intelligence looks and sounds like, but to do so in way that makes sense to teachers, and which gives them practical ways of thinking about how they might help those contributory habits of mind to grow stronger, and to interweave in ever more subtle and effective ways. So although descriptions such as Costa and Kallick's are based on scientific research, they are driven by educational considerations as well.

We have also been involved in creating and publishing different variations of such lists. When Bill was Chief Executive of the Campaign for Learning, he initiated the Learning to Learn research projects with an expanding number of UK schools that worked with a system called the 5Rs. They were:

1 *Readiness to learn*: being emotionally and practically ready and willing to learn something and believing you can do it.

2 *Resourcefulness*: knowing how to use different approaches to learning.

3 *Resilience*: being able to cope with difficulty and bounce back from frustration and error.

4 *Remembering*: being able to recall different learning strategies which you have used in other contexts.

5 *Reflectiveness*: being able to stand back, take stock, and think about your own thinking.[12]

You'll see that these differ somewhat from Costa and Kallick's habits of mind, but overlap with them to a considerable extent.

The Campaign for Learning approach was based partly on the system that Guy had been developing, in his work with schools, called Building Learning Power, or BLP for short.[13] The BLP orchestra can be divided into four main sections – resilience, resourcefulness, reflection and relationships – in which three of the four Rs correspond to those listed above. But BLP also unpacks each of those Rs into four or five more specific 'learning muscles',[14] as they are called, which give a level of detail closer to that of Costa and Kallick.

Again, there are strong similarities. Both BLP and Habits of Mind emphasize the importance of being able to stick with difficulty; of being able to stand back and reflect; of empathy and listening; of balancing rigorous thinking with imagination; of being able both to collaborate with others and to think independently; and of being able to immerse yourself in experience and allow wonder to crystallize into good questions. But the BLP learning muscles also include the ability to concentrate – to 'manage distractions' so that your focus of attention is not disturbed – as well as the ability to capitalize on the material resources around to create an effective 'learning support system' for yourself. BLP also tries to help young learners to be good eavesdroppers and observers of how other people around them are going about learning, so that they are on the alert to pick up useful strategies and approaches to enrich their own repertoire.

In the booklet called *New Kinds of Smart*[15] to which we referred in the Prelude, we, along with others from the UK's Talent Foundation, have taken a slightly different approach in describing those aspects of intelligence – we have called them the '16 elements' – for which there is evidence that supports both their validity and learnability. Inevitably there is overlap with the other orchestral approaches we have been describing, although concepts like 'goal orientation', 'openness to experience', 'intuitive thinking' and 'social intuition' add some new instrumental possibilities.

Clearly, identifying the instruments that go to make up the orchestra of intelligence is a work-in-progress. Nevertheless, there is sufficient agreement to enable educators to start thinking about how the idea of composite intelligence can make a difference to the way they go about organizing teaching and learning.

Starting out

To begin with, the idea of composite intelligence found its way into a good many schools through attempts to operationalize Gardner's MI framework, as well as through the idea of learning styles. When teachers were used to thinking of intelligence as a unitary, fixed commodity, it was almost second nature for them to see students as occupying their own spot on the scale from 'bright' to 'dim'. While they subscribed, consciously or not, to the assumptions that lay behind this unidimensional scale 'ability', educators often felt rather uncomfortable about placing individual students at the bottom end, and sought a succession of euphemisms to avoid having to come out and call someone 'stupid'. So sometimes they were 'lower ability', sometimes 'slow', sometimes 'one of our weaker ones', sometimes 'an improver'. But with the advent of MI and learning styles, it became possible to situate students not along a single line, but in terms of a more variegated profile.

Often MI theory – partly, perhaps, due to Gardner's own ambivalence on the issue – was interpreted as replacing the one fixed dimension with eight fixed dimensions. Young people's genes condemned them, not just to a spot on a line, but to a profile of different spots on eight different lines. Emma could be high in linguistic and

> "When teachers were used to thinking of intelligence as a unitary, fixed commodity, it was almost second nature for them to see students as occupying their own spot on the scale from 'bright' to 'dim'. While they subscribed, consciously or not, to the assumptions that lay behind this unidimensional scale 'ability', educators often felt rather uncomfortable about placing individual students at the bottom end, and sought a succession of euphemisms to avoid having to come out and call someone 'stupid'."

inter-personal intelligence, average in logical-mathematical and musical, and low in bodily-kinaesthetic, intra-personal and spatial, for example. The hope was that students who had not been blessed with the intelligences traditionally valued by school – linguistic and logical-mathematical – could nevertheless derive some 'self-esteem' from being good at hockey or relationships, because they provided evidence of 'intelligence', and intelligence is a valued attribute. In some schools, this manoeuvre was successful, but in others, the multiple intelligences were immediately overlaid with a traditional hierarchy of esteem, so that it was clear to everyone that though all intelligences were equal, as George Orwell put it in *Animal Farm*, some were much more equal than others. Bodily-kinaesthetic intelligence and inter-personal intelligence were much admired, yet the intelligences behind gymnastics and kindness still seemed to count for less than those behind quadratic equations and essay-writing. (MI has not translated into schools being judged on eight different league tables or sets of performance indicators, for example, rather than just the one.)

Even schools that hoped that it might be possible to help their students improve on the eight intelligences – to get smarter in eight different ways – often fell into the trap of using 'multiple intelligences' as new lesson content, to be thought about, remembered and recited in ways that seemed to require only the same old logical and linguistic mental skills. We have observed lessons, for example, where Year 9s were parroting back simplistic formulae for each of the 'intelligences', and being asked to 'discuss them' in rather narrow terms. So instead of valuing and developing intra-personal and spatial intelligence, say, they were simply being treated as more material to be learned and recalled – and that kind of limited understanding and rote retention is very unlikely to translate into students actually developing different ways of using their minds.

Going deeper

Richer and more comprehensive descriptions of the orchestra of intelligence can help teachers to think about how to plan their lessons. The series of books by Costa and Kallick,[16] for example, are full of ideas about how the habits of mind can be brought more fully into lessons. Let us just give a flavour of the approach here from the work of teachers in the UK who have been experimenting with the Building Learning Power framework.

A useful tool: the 'split screen lesson'

This is a lesson that is planned to have two complementary objectives.

One relates to the content: the skill or knowledge that the teacher wants her students to acquire. The second relates to the 'learning muscle' – the aspect of learnable intelligence – that she wants them to exercise, and so strengthen, as they work on the topic.

Both objectives are clearly displayed and referred to throughout the lesson.

A Year 6 class is embarking on a science lesson. The topic is magnets. Their teacher, Miss Green, has laid out round the classroom a circus of experiments she wants the children to carry out. They are to go around in groups of three, follow the instructions on the cards, and observe how the magnets behave. So far, so familiar. However, as she settles them down, Miss Green is talking to the children about 'which learning muscle they are going to be stretching today'. She refers to the line strung across her classroom to which are pegged a number of laminated cards, each of which describes one of the 'learning muscles' (with which the children are increasingly familiar). She tells them that she wants them to work on their 'questioning muscles', and explains that their task, once they have carried out each little experiment, is to see if they can think of the kinds of questions that a scientist might want to ask next. 'As you see how the magnets behave, what does that make you wonder?', she explains.

At the end of the lesson, she draws the groups of pupils back together to share both their observations and their questions; and then she encourages the children to discuss what makes a good scientist's question, and how you can tell. Soon the children are involved in a vigorous discussion about falsifiability and the nature of evidence – though they have not been introduced to those terms yet. As they leave the lesson, they have learned something about magnets – and they have also sharpened their understanding that there are different kinds of questions that are 'good' for different kinds of tasks.

Now let's move to a Year 8 History lesson. They are 'doing the Tudors'. They have been learning about Queen Elizabeth I and Mary Queen of Scots, and the machinations of the royal court. Now their teacher, Mrs Price, has asked them to write about a critical event – but to do so through the eyes of different protagonists. They are asked to imagine how it looks to Elizabeth, to Mary, and to Lord Burleigh, Elizabeth's most trusted Minister of State. She encourages them, metaphorically, to 'put on their empathy specs', and try to

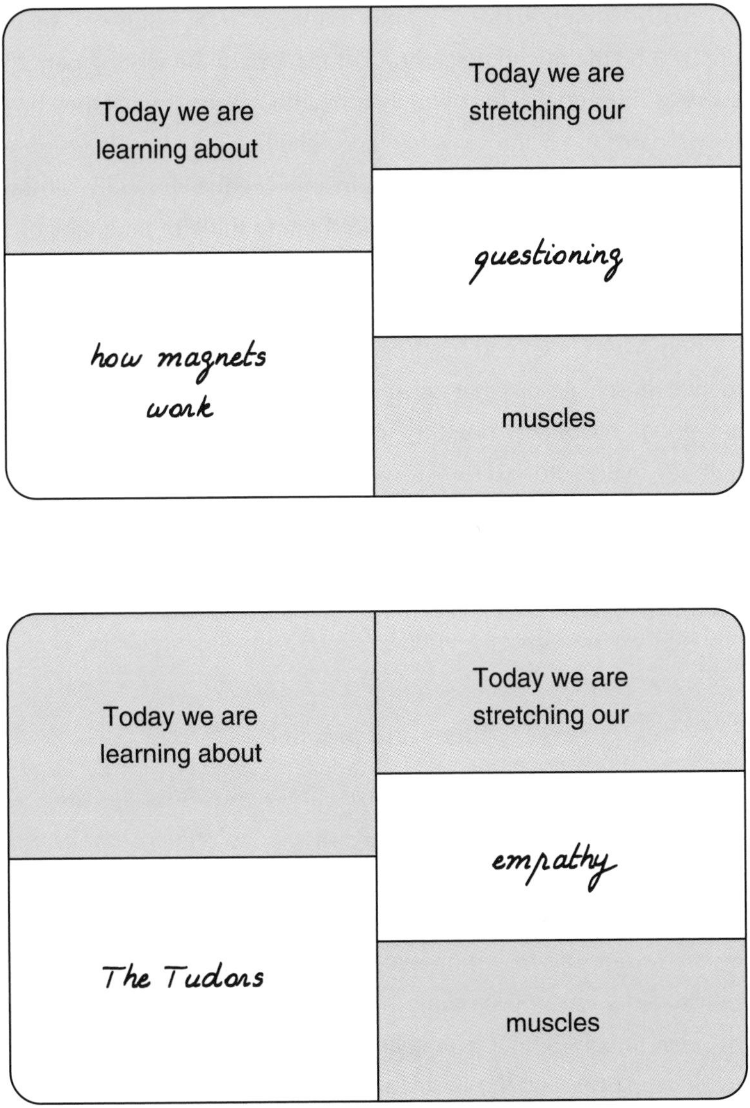

Figure 1.1 The Split Screen Lesson

imagine as vividly as possible how things looked and felt to the three people, each holding very different views. She says she wants them to 'really stretch those empathy muscles'. (The students seem unfazed by the mixed metaphor!) At the end of the writing period, she asks the students to talk to their neighbour about what they had found hard about the exercise, and whether they had been able to hold the different perspectives in mind, equally vividly, at the same time. For homework, she asks them to think of an analogous situation in their own lives, and to write a short play showing the views of the three participants through their own words.

Both Miss Green and Mrs Price have an overview of the different mental muscle groups that together go to make up intelligence. Like any good coach, they don't try to exercise all the muscles at once, but they make sure that they vary the habits of mind which they are asking students to bring into play, so that, over a term or a year, they get a good all-round mental workout. And they make sure to share their map of composite intelligence with the students, and discuss and improve it as they go along.

Ideas into practice

In sample lessons like these, we can see how teachers are making use of the vocabulary of the constituent habits and frames of mind to construct activities that serve two purposes. There is no question of throwing out the content in favour of the emphasis on the process of learning. Students are still learning their history and their science. The only difference is that the content is being used imaginatively as the basis for a 'work-out' for each of the learning muscles in turn.

To help you think how you might try out ideas about composite intelligence, you might like to wonder:[17]

1 Which of the ideas in this chapter strike me as having the most practical utility? Are there some that seem too theoretical to me, at the moment, to see how I can make use of them? Would it be worth sharing some possibilities with a colleague?

2 How could I try to help my learners become more self-disciplined? Are there any stories I could share with them about how that kind of self-control has helped me or other people achieve their goals?

3 How could using language like 'habits of mind' or 'learning muscles' change my practice? Might students have a different take on difficulty if they saw it as a 'mental workout'?

4 How could I plan lessons that both teach the necessary subject content and at the same time exercise the different 'learning muscles' in turn? Which of the habits of mind, say, might be easiest to have a go at?

5 Could I give students more responsibility to design their own mental workouts, selecting for themselves which aspects of their intelligence they wanted to try to improve?

6 What would be the best way to discuss these ideas with colleagues so that I can engage both 'traditional' teachers and those who are already more in tune with these kinds of ideas?

7 Are there any aspects of my own thinking, or my own habitual ways of doing things, that might make it difficult for me to incorporate some of the thinking in this chapter into my teaching?

As we have suggested, you might like to pursue some of these trains of thought on your own. Others might work well as a discussion among colleagues, or even directly with your students. What do you think?

2

Intelligence is Expandable

Some recent philosophers have given their moral approval
to the deplorable verdict that an individual's intelligence
is a fixed quantity, one which cannot be augmented. We
must protest and act against this brutal pessimism . . . it
has no foundation whatsoever . . . What [slow learners]
should learn first is not the subjects ordinarily taught,
however important they may be; they should be given
lessons of will, of attention, of discipline; before exercises
in grammar, they need to be exercised in mental
orthopedics; in a word they must learn how to learn.

Alfred Binet[1]

Good news. You can become more intelligent by believing that you can become
more intelligent! This is the exciting finding
of a major research programme by Stanford
professor Carol Dweck and colleagues.[2]
In one study, Dweck took a group of

> **"Good news. You can
> become more intelligent by
> believing that you can
> become more intelligent!"**
> adapted from Carol Dweck

33

12-year-olds in New York and, over the course of eight weeks, spent a total of three hours teaching them about the expandability of intelligence, persuading them that their brains were more like a growing muscle than a fixed-sized pot, and encouraging them to see their learning as a matter of effort and strategy rather than 'ability'. At the end of the course, their engagement and their mathematical understanding were compared with a group who had been taught about memory strategies – but not about the malleability of intelligence – for the same length of time. The first group had significantly raised their intelligent engagement with their learning; the latter group had not. With just three hours' worth of information and encouragement, these students had got smarter.

Pondering on how such a relatively small intervention could have such a positive effect on students in spite of the wide range of their backgrounds, Dweck speculates that much of the effect of those backgrounds is distilled into the mental attitudes and self-beliefs they have come to possess. And this 'mental baggage', as she calls it, can be addressed, and altered, directly.

Getting to grips with expandable intelligence

As we saw in the last chapter, it is interesting to note that the founder of IQ, Alfred Binet, did not believe that intelligence was a unitary faculty, separate from other aspects of a person's psychology. But neither did he believe that intelligence was a fixed commodity. As the quotation which starts this chapter shows, he was aware of the danger that his tests might be used to support the 'brutal pessimism' of fixed intelligence, and was passionate that people should not fall into the trap. History sadly records that thousands of educators, as well as many parents, policy-makers and media pundits, have subsequently proved only too keen to make the mistake that Binet warned so clearly against. As a result, many children suffer the daily abuse of being treated as if their learning successes and failures were a reliable guide to the unalterable, generic capacity of their minds (provided, of course, that they 'tried').

> **"Many children suffer the daily abuse of being treated as if their learning successes and failures were a reliable guide to the unalterable, generic capacity of their minds."**

Some of the blame for this situation has to lie with a deep misunderstanding of the relationship between nature and nurture. The early studies of the 'heritability' of intelligence assumed that you could separate the proportion that was fixed – predetermined by your genetic make-up – and the proportion that was left free to be influenced by your own individual experience. But this simple-minded cleaving of the two sets of influences does not reflect reality. Genes do not express themselves willy-nilly, establishing a deterministic biological cage that defines and limits your room to grow and develop. On the contrary, experience plays a powerful role in determining how and when the genes themselves are going to be expressed. Let Matt Ridley[3] explain:

> To appreciate what has happened [in recent science] you will have to abandon cherished notions and open your mind. You will have to enter a world where your genes are no puppet-masters, pulling the strings of your behaviour, but are themselves puppets at the mercy of your behaviour; a world where instinct is not the opposite of learning, where environmental influences are sometimes less reversible than genetic ones, and where nature is designed for nurture . . . Genes are designed to take their cues from nurture.

> "There are genetic influences on intelligence, but they are very far from being a life sentence. And they are not large."

So there are genetic influences on intelligence, but they are very far from being a life sentence. And they are not large. Recent research by behavioural geneticist Robert Plomin, of the University of London's Institute of Psychiatry, has identified six genes that are strongly associated with high or low measured intelligence. Taken together, they account for just 1 per cent of the variation in intelligence.[4] At most, genes seem to establish a broad 'envelope of possibility' which is heavily modified and influenced by experience. What is of interest to geneticists now is not the discovery of some crude biological determinism, but the uncovering of all the subtle ways in which genes get turned on and off, up and down, by the biochemical environment in which they find themselves; and all the ways in which that bodily environment is powerfully and continually being modified by experience and behaviour. There truly is no scientific justification any more – if there ever was – for labelling children as having different amounts of 'intelligence', 'ability', or even – the new weasely euphemism – 'potential'.

> "There truly is no scientific justification any more – if there ever was – for labelling children as having different amounts of 'intelligence, 'ability', or even – the new weasely euphemism – 'potential'."

Of course, none of this is to deny that children differ in their current levels of achievement or performance (their CLAPs, we call them) in all kinds of ways – as we all do. Take any group of learners, and some of them will be better than others at anything you care to name. You can even argue that, under some circumstances, it would be effective and helpful to group them according to their CLAPs – as happens in athletics clubs and dance classes wherever you go. But this is a pragmatic question of how best to help them all improve. It need say nothing at all about how far they might ultimately go. And that is what the gratuitous addition of the 'ability' label does: it takes people's CLAPs and turns them into fatalistic predictions about what can be expected of them. And there is no scientific justification for doing that.

Growth mindsets

There is another argument about whether intelligence is fixed or expandable that is even more important than the scientific one. As our opening piece of research showed, it matters whether people *believe* that their own intelligence is fixed or expandable. Whether they know it or not, some people tend to think that they were born with a fixed-capacity mental engine that determines how far and how fast they can go. Other people tend to believe that their minds are like their bodies: they come in different shapes and sizes, but everyone can get a good deal fitter and stronger. Their mental muscles benefit from exercise, and the more they stretch their brains, the stronger and more flexible their brains will be. (Of course the brain isn't a muscle; this is just a metaphor.) Carol Dweck, with whose research we began this chapter, has shown, over more than 20 years of study, that the effects of these contrasting beliefs on how people go about learning is considerable.

To pursue the physical analogy, people who believe that their minds, like their bodies, can get fitter and stronger with exercise, tend to enjoy challenges that stretch them. They like pushing themselves,

> ❝People who believe that their minds, like their bodies, can get fitter and stronger with exercise, tend to enjoy challenges that stretch them.❞

37

> "People who think that their minds are fixed, on the other hand, are more likely to see challenges as a threat to their supposed level of ability, and shy away from situations where they might look and feel 'stupid'."

because, at the back of their minds is the belief that struggling with difficulty is usually profitable. They are not bothered if someone else finds what they are struggling with easy – they are competing with themselves, not with the person on the exercise bike, or the desk, beside them. People who think that their minds are fixed, on the other hand, are more likely to see challenges as a threat to their supposed level of ability, and shy away from situations where they might look and feel 'stupid'. They don't like having to try, or making mistakes, because they interpret that as showing that their fixed-sized pot of intelligence is inadequate. They are more likely to avoid such challenges, get upset, or, if all else fails, cheat.

Where do these different mindsets come from? Largely, so Dweck has found, from the way parents, teachers and older children respond to a young person's successes, struggles and failures. Like the flu, these belief systems turn out to be highly contagious. If kids are praised for being smart, they are likely to fall prey to the 'trying to look good' mindset. If they are encouraged to persist, try hard, enjoy difficulty, and look for new strategies, they are much more likely to develop the 'mind is a muscle' attitude. As Carol Dweck says in her book *Mindset*:[5]

> "If parents want to give their children a gift, the best thing they can do is teach their children to love challenges, be intrigued by mistakes, enjoy effort, and keep on learning."
>
> Carol Dweck

If parents want to give their children a gift, the best thing they can do is teach their children to love challenges, be intrigued by mistakes, enjoy effort, and keep on learning. That way their children don't have to be slaves of praise. They will have a lifelong way to build and repair their own confidence.

Lauren Resnick, the doyenne of American intelligence researchers, sums it up:

> Students who, over an extended period of time are treated as if they are intelligent, actually become more so. If they are taught demanding content, and are expected to explain and find connections . . . they learn more and learn more quickly. They [come to] think of themselves as learners. They are [better] able to bounce back in the face of short-term failures.[6]

So the key to expandable intelligence lies far more in self-belief than it does in any hypothetical underlying notion of 'ability'. This self-belief goes by a variety of names in the psychological literature. Carol Dweck calls it 'growth mindset' or 'mastery orientation'. It is the deep-down belief, born of experience, that putting in the effort of learning is a worthwhile thing to do, because it is likely to bear fruit both in terms of making progress on things you care about, and in terms of strengthening intelligence itself, which will stand you in good stead in the future. She opposes this to the 'fixed mindset' or 'helpless prone orientation', in which effort feels painful and often pointless, because you *don't* believe that it will pay off.

> "Students who, over an extended period of time are treated as if they are intelligent, actually become more so. If they are taught demanding content, and are expected to explain and find connections . . . they learn more and learn more quickly."
>
> Lauren Resnick

These belief systems are not necessarily conscious, but they are readily revealed both through the patterns to which they give rise, and through direct answers to simple questions like: 'Do you think it is possible to get smarter, or do you think we are just born with a certain amount of smart?'

Positive psychology

Albert Bandura's concept of *self-efficacy*,[7] and Julian Rotter's idea of *locus of control*,[8] are related to this idea – they both refer to whether you think that what you do can make a significant difference, or whether you are just the victim of events that are beyond your control. And there is a good deal of evidence in the field known as 'positive psychology' that optimism – the belief that things will, on the whole, go well for you rather than badly – is related to people's happiness, their engagement in life and projects, and even the way their immune systems respond to stress.[9]

Martin Seligman, the father of the positive psychology movement, coined the phrase 'learned optimism'[10] to describe the positive mind set which we can all cultivate and which will help us to be more successful in learning and life. Seligman suggests that the world is divided into two kinds of people. One group are optimists, the other are pessimists. It all comes down to the way you account for things that happen to you, your 'explanatory style'. Seligman describes this as having three elements: permanence, pervasiveness and personalization, the 3 Ps.

Have you ever wondered why people who seem to be very similarly intelligent can have very different dispositions towards what needs to be done? Some are 'glass half-full' people, always seeing the bright side of a problem while others are 'glass half-empty'. (American comedienne Joan Rivers claims to be so much of a pessimist that it isn't even a matter of the glass being half-empty: somebody stole the glass.) Some are only knocked back for a few moments when something goes wrong and rapidly evolve a way of seeing it as an isolated misfortune, where others immediately make it part of a pattern of failure and bad luck. The 3 Ps help to explain this.

> *Permanence*: When things go wrong, optimists see this as a one-off setback, pessimists as something that always happens. A pessimist would think 'Things like this ALWAYS happen to me and the effects go on for ever.'
>
> *Pervasiveness*: When things go wrong, optimists realize it was because of a particular situation, pessimists see it spreading right through their lives. A pessimist would say 'Things like this ALWAYS happen to me and that's typical of everything I do in my life.'
>
> *Personalization*: When things go wrong, optimists take control of events, pessimists sink into a depression imagining that the whole world is against them. A pessimist would say 'Things like this always happen to ME.'

Behaviourist theory suggests that you are a victim of your environment and situation. The concept of learned optimism and its associated techniques show that this need not be the case; for your intelligence is expandable. Learned optimism, like learnable intelligence is, in a sense, the opposite of the learned helplessness or learning powerlessness that is all too often on show in school, where pupils have succumbed to a limiting belief that they have

> "Learned optimism, like learnable intelligence is, in a sense, the opposite of the learned helplessness or learning powerlessness that is all too often on show in school, where pupils have succumbed to a limiting belief that they have little personal power to change their lot in life; that their own effort will not count for much."

little personal power to change their lot in life; that their own effort will not count for much.

The previous chapter gave us some ideas about what intelligence might be made up of – the different instruments in the orchestra of intelligence. This chapter suggests that each of these instruments is capable of being played better; or, to use a different metaphor, each of the threads that go to make up the complex fabric of intelligence is itself capable of being strengthened. But what exactly is it that is being strengthened? Thinking about this has changed since the late 1990s.

Starting out

In the early days of the study of 'learning-to-learn', people wondered if making people smarter was a matter of giving them *techniques* and *strategies* – for managing their time, or organizing their lecture notes, for example. But it quickly became obvious that, while these 'hints and tips' can be useful in certain circumstances, they didn't really add up to a deep expansion of all-round intelligence. For example, they often related mainly to school-based concerns like retrieving facts for an examination, or organizing your revision schedule. For example, you can teach students to draw spidery diagrams (sometimes called 'mind-maps' or 'concept maps') that show how ideas are connected to each other and help them haul that cluster of ideas up out of memory; but no one would really claim that this useful little technique was the key to living a fulfilled and happy life.

So the study of expandable intelligence moved on and became a search for teachable or trainable *skills*. Courses were designed to teach 'thinking skills', 'critical skills', and so on. Students were trained, through a variety of games and exercises, to be able to argue more rationally by detecting logical flaws in other people's arguments and considering counter-arguments to their own positions, for example. They learned how to use Edward de Bono's 'Six Thinking Hats'[11] to be more imaginative, sceptical or information-seeking. Often these ideas were well received by students, and did indeed show that, in the context of these courses, the quality of their thinking had improved. However, on closer inspection, the results were less encouraging. Often these improvements were found not to last, and not to transfer to other situations. David Perkins, who has done a lot of research in this area, has shown that often skills acquired in this way are *inert*: that is, they can be *called* to mind when they are directly prompted, but do not *come* to mind spontaneously when they might be needed.[12]

These results reveal a potential flaw when it comes to thinking about intelligence as being made up of *skills*. For 'skills' are something you *can* do, but are not necessarily what you *do* do. The answer to the question 'Can you play the piano?' may well be different from the answer to 'Do you play the piano?' And, to revert to our previous analogy, it is not much use having a full symphony orchestra of intelligent instruments in your head if half of them are kept 'locked in a cupboard' and never get played. So we have to think of intelligence as being composed not of skills but of dispositions or what we have earlier called *habits of mind*. Thus, one aspect of being smart is being ready, willing and able to be curious

> ❝One aspect of being smart is being ready, willing and able to be curious and ask questions. Another is being ready, willing and able to use your imagination in different ways. Another is being ready, willing and able to persist in the face of difficulty.❞

and ask questions. Another is being ready, willing and able to use your imagination in different ways. Another is being ready, willing and able to persist in the face of difficulty. And so on.

So if we are going to try to help young people expand their intelligence, we have to be in the business, not of training skills, but of *cultivating dispositions*. We have to be looking for ways to help them become more ready and more willing to make use of their mental instruments, as well as better able to play them. 'Being ready' means being on the look-out for opportunities to question, persist and be imaginative. You don't wait for the world to give you a hefty nudge; you are dispositionally curious and determined. So helping someone develop readiness means helping them to develop what Perkins calls 'sensitivity to occasion'. And that means giving them a broad range of experiences in which to question, persist, reason and imagine, so those habits of mind become relatively disembedded from specific tasks and materials, and more general-purpose.

'Being willing' means being inclined to make use of each of the habits, even though there may not be strong support for doing so. Having a strong disposition to question means you can't *not* ask questions, even when your teacher is gasping for a coffee-break, or your coach is getting harassed and short-tempered. The disposition becomes more and more robust. So to help someone develop that robustness, you have to gradually stop prompting and encouraging them, and get them to the point where the habits of mind are second nature: part of their make-up.

And 'being able' is the skilful part. An able imaginer or questioner is one who is rich and flexible in their use of their imagination and their curiosity. They have the fluidity and the variability of the expert, able to phrase their questions well and to use their imagination differently for different purposes. So helping someone become a more skilful reasoner, say, involves helping them develop a range of different strategies and approaches they can draw on as needed.

Another early and understandable approach to teaching expandable intelligence was the belief that praising children is always a good thing. Praising learners is good, the argument goes, because it boosts their self-esteem, gives them confidence and shows you value them. It is easy to see why these kinds of beliefs grew up. Indeed, at first glance they seem universally benign.

But go beneath the surface and you find that praising learners is not always such a good idea. For example, if you are praised for doing things you found easy, the praise may reinforce a belief in the fixity of intelligence and imply, albeit subtly, that the expenditure of effort is unlikely to be beneficial. ('Smart people don't break sweat.') Conversely, if specifically commended for aspects of your effort which have led to improvement, then the message is clear; certain kinds of effort contribute to making you more intelligent. Too much praise, especially where it is in effect simply congratulating you for being clever, can be harmful. It can encourage a kind of

> **"Too much praise, especially where it is in effect simply congratulating you for being clever, can be harmful. It can encourage a kind of mindlessly competitive culture that helps to ensure the continuation of fixed mindsets rather than the cultivation of learners who believe that their intelligence is malleable."**

mindlessly competitive culture that helps to ensure the continuation of fixed mindsets rather than the cultivation of learners who believe that their intelligence is malleable.

Some critics have gone further,[13] citing the praise culture as a sign of the times in which, in a misplaced attempt to help our children think that they are special, we have lost the ability to notice when real effort is taking place. Instead we are bringing up an over-praised generation who continue to seek our praise rather than figuring out what they really need to do to pursue their own dreams and passions.

Going deeper

Thinking about how schools can expand intelligence is in its infancy, and, not surprisingly, there is not yet much reliable practice on which to draw. Carol Dweck has worked on the intervention in schools we described at the beginning of this chapter called 'Brainology', which introduces students to the idea of expandable intelligence. Interestingly she has targeted seventh grade students (Year 8 in the UK) at a time when they may be turning off school.[14] The workshop starts by offering students a new metaphor for their brains and how they work:

> "When they do think about what intelligence is, many people believe that a person is born either smart, average or dumb – and stays that way for life. But new research shows that the brain is more like a muscle – it changes and gets stronger when you use it."
>
> Carol Dweck

Many people think of the brain as a mystery. They don't know much about intelligence and how it works. When they do think about what intelligence is, many people believe that a person is born either smart, average or dumb – and stays that way for life. But new research shows that the brain is more like a muscle – it changes and gets stronger when you use it. And scientists have been able to show just how the brain grows and gets stronger when you learn.

Dweck goes on to explain how the brain literally changes and grows by making new connections – neural pathways. Eight sessions with a range of activities then follow. These allow students to see just how much their own self-belief influences their performance and, therefore, why effort really matters. Students are essentially being told that they are in charge of their minds and, perhaps not surprisingly, their performance, especially in mathematics, improved significantly.

There are many interventions around that encourage schools to try to strengthen specific groups of 'learning muscles'. Art Costa and Bena Kallick's habits of mind and Guy Claxton's Building Learning Power approach are full of practical suggestions about how students' brains can be stretched, and they both focus on trying to build up a strong, lasting culture in the school, rather than just adding a few 'hints and tips', or falling into the trap of ignoring the importance of developing minds that are 'ready' and 'willing' as well as 'able'. Because these approaches are relatively new, there are many case studies of successful intervention, but as yet few large-scale independent evaluations of their effectiveness. Developing these is an important next step.

A useful tool: expansive talking

Here are a set of questions which teachers find useful in helping learners to focus on the degree to which they can grow:

- What's going well?
- Which was the hardest bit?
- How did you deal with it?
- How else could you have done it?
- What could you do when you are stuck on that?
- What would have made that easier for you?
- What mistakes did you make that you can learn from?
- Is there anything else you know that might help?
- How could you help someone else do that?
- How could I have taught that better?
- Where else could I use that?
- How could you make that harder for yourself?
- How did it feel when you had finished?

Ideas into practice

For a long while schools have been governed by two notions: attainment and effort – how bright you are and how hard you try. It turns out that there is a third one –

mindset – how bright you think you are and how much you believe that effort matters.

To help you think about how you might try out ideas about expandable intelligence, and the role of mindsets, you might like to wonder:

1   Should I rethink my use of praise and what it is intended to achieve? When do I praise my students, and what, really, am I trying to achieve? Could I shift the focus on my praise and encouragement from their products to their processes and levels of engagement?

2   Deep down, how much do I really subscribe to the fixed view of intelligence? Do I sometimes talk in terms of fixed levels of 'ability', even if I'm not sure about the validity of the underlying view of the mind? How hard would it be to change any long-held views of intelligence I might hold? What would help me to do so?

3   How could I set up a similar experiment with students to the one Carol Dweck devised? Could I talk to them about their brains being like muscles that get stronger with exercise?

4   Would using the idea of 'dispositions' help me when talking about these ideas with colleagues? Could I use the idea of helping students to become more ready and more willing, as well as more able, to use different aspects of their intelligence? What would that look like in my classroom?

5   Are some dispositions or habits of mind more

important than others? What could I do to come up with an answer to this question?

6 What is the best way for me to help young people develop a growth mindset in the context of their out-of-school learning? Are there opportunities for me to help them bridge between the worlds of school and home?

7 What could I do to help parents cultivate growth mindsets in their children? Are there notes we could send home to encourage parents to notice and praise effort more than achievement?

8 Could we use report-writing as a way of helping students see themselves as expanding their intelligence? Could we get better at capturing and celebrating aspects of their mental growth?

3

Intelligence is Practical

The hand is the cutting edge of the mind.

Jacob Bronowski[1]

Two hunters in the woods are suddenly confronted by a huge grizzly bear. One immediately gropes in his pack for his trainers and slips them on. The other says scornfully, 'You don't think you can outrun an adult grizzly, do you?' 'No,' says the first, 'All I have to do is outrun you.'[2]

The great mathematician Alan Turing was exceedingly bright by anyone's standards. He spent World War II cracking 'unbreakable' German codes, and is considered by many to be the father of computer science. He had a bicycle on which he rode to work every day in Cambridge, and every so often the chain would fall off. He kept a bottle of turpentine and a rag in his office with which to clean his oily hands. After a while, he noticed that the chain fell off after an exact number of revolutions of the front wheel. He developed a particular manoeuvre that, if executed at the right moment, would prevent the mishap, but he had to count the wheel revolutions accurately for this to work. As this counting stopped him thinking as he rode, he fixed a counter to the wheel that would do the job for him. On further investigation, he uncovered a precise mathematical relationship between the size of the front wheel, the number of links in the chain, and the number of cogs on the pedal. The chain fell off only when there was a unique configuration of wheel, chain and pedals. Yet more study revealed that the chain fell off when a particular damaged link in the chain met a particular bent cog on the pedal. So, after months of brilliant investigation and deduction, he straightened the cog, fixed the problem, and drank the turpentine. (Only kidding!) A bike mechanic would have diagnosed and fixed the problem in five minutes. As the mathematician Ian Stewart comments, after recounting this story in the science journal *Nature*, 'This tale illustrates both the power and the perils of logical reasoning.'[3]

The difference between academic and practical intelligence is part of folk-lore. It is embodied in the idea of the absent-minded professor (of which the Turing story is an example), and American humorist H.L. Mencken's observation that 'There's no idea so stupid that you can't find a professor who believes it.' And it is amply demonstrated by research. Take Stephen Ceci and Jeff Liker's study of horse-race handicappers called 'A day at the races'.[4] They identified a group of American bookies who were reliably expert at setting the odds, and tried to uncover how they did it. They found that the experts took into account around seven different variables. They intuitively assigned different weights to these factors. And the weights they assigned to one factor were influenced by the values of the other factors. For example, they looked at the horse's 'form' in previous races in great detail: how they ran the race, how far off the rails they tended to run, how quickly they came out of the starting gates, their speed over the final furlong, their performance relative to the eventual winner, and what the 'going' had been like. If the going had been 'firm', that would adjust the weightings they gave to the speed over the final furlong – and so on.

In statistical terms, what they are computing in their heads – and not necessarily very consciously or explicitly – are seven-factor multiplicative models involving multiple interaction and regression effects. A small computer would get out of breath doing these. Ceci and Liker then gave the bookies a battery of intelligence tests, and examined the correlation between their scores on these and their handicapping prowess. There was no relation. Their IQ score was irrelevant in predicting the success of their very complex thinking at the race track.

Getting to grips with practical intelligence

Nobody knows where the students who progress through the school system end up. (In the British school system this amounts to some 600,000 a year.) Some will become professors of philosophy, and will need those razor-sharp intellectual skills of analysis and argumentation, but very few. The rest will benefit from being able to think things through carefully, when they need to, and being able to discuss topics and resolve conflicts in a calm and reasonable way. They will, of course, need a certain level of those logical, analytical skills – and it is therefore very curious that schools on the whole don't even do a very good job of developing those.[5] But they will also need all the other ingredients of an all-round intelligent mind which we are discussing, and none more so than those that involve hands-on engagement with the real world of horses, bicycles and practical arrangements of all kinds. They will need to be smart with their eyes, hands and feelings, as well as with their abstract rational minds. An IQ of 150 will not necessarily help them fix their bike in the quickest and easiest way; sometimes, as with Alan Turing, the reverse.

> "The sad fact is that schools perpetuate a kind of snobbery about practical and bodily intelligence that has been with us a long time, and that is well past its think-by date."

The sad fact is that schools perpetuate a kind of snobbery about practical and bodily intelligence that has been with us a long time, and that is well past its think-by date. From the time of Plato, down through the mainstream Christian tradition, to Descartes and beyond, Western societies have valued the abstract over the concrete, the intellectual over the practical. The body is subject to emotion and decay; it is impermanent and unreliable; its knowledge and skills always fallible. So certainty and purity were sought in the abstractions and idealizations of Religion and Reason. Bishops and mathematicians both claimed that their Knowledge was better – pristine, timeless and incorruptible – and it is not so long since most teachers stopped wearing the gowns and hoods that signalled the origin of their authority in the monastery and seminary. The rational mind was the human faculty that distinguished us most from the brutes, and so it was in mental activity that our intelligence was most evident. The body, by contrast, was menial and simple. Human meat could no more be called 'intelligent' than could the flesh of cattle and pigs.

So it was to the development of rationality that education directed itself – first for the elite, and then for all. And Physical Education and Woodwork were for those who sadly lacked the mental raw material to benefit. School subjects were ordered, in terms of attention and esteem, from the most ethereal to the most physical, with Algebra, Geometry, Mathematical Physics and Grammar at the top, through languages and humanities, to the arts, and down to anything that might make you physically tired, bruised, dusty or muddy at the bottom (with the exception of a few sports that required the particular kinds of bravery, strength and fellowship with which a certain kind of 'well-bred gentleman' was associated). Despite many attempts to correct it, that snobbery still badly affects many systems today, with those colleges providing further and vocational education and apprenticeships being seen as somehow second class.

The emerging science of embodied cognition

However, the emerging discipline of embodied cognition is helping to correct and expand our idea of intelligence. Though brains look quite uninteresting to the naked eye, neuroscience now tells us just how astonishingly smart they are. We will see in the next chapter how brains underwrite much of human creativity. But it is not just brains that are smart; research is implicating the body too. Bodies are not, as Ken Robinson[6] has joked, merely an intellectual's way of getting their mind to a meeting. Nor do they just provide the channels though which our intelligence expresses itself. They are vital ingredients of our intelligence. Contrary to what Descartes thought, bodies *are* intelligent.

Embodied cognition as a field is developing fast, and there is not space in this short book to do justice to it. We shall have to make do with illustrating three of the constituent areas of research:

1 Smart ways of learning physical skills and expertise.

2   Smart ways of making things and working with your hands.

3   Smart ways of understanding bodily feelings and emotions.

Each of these areas makes a vital contribution to a rich and fulfilled human life; and each, as we shall see, requires a broader, and in some cases different, set of habits of mind than are required to do well in public examinations such as the UK's GCSEs and A levels, the International Baccalaureate or any other similar assessment.

Developing practical expertise

> **"**Piaget is reported to have defined intelligence as 'knowing what to do when you don't know what to do'.**"**

Piaget is reported to have defined intelligence as 'knowing what to do when you don't know what to do'. So what is it that smart people know when they want to get better at a physical skill? What does it take to practise intelligently?

Take someone practising the cello. Do they know what time of day they practise best? Can they tell you what a 'good' practice session feels like? How long do they practise for? Do they set a time and stick to it, or do they take a break when they are tired, or getting frustrated? How well do they monitor or respond to changes in their mood or concentration? Do they start with exercises and scales, or go straight to the pieces – and why? Do they work at getting the technique mastered before developing the interpretation, or work on both together? How do they identify what the 'hard parts' are, and what is the balance between working on those versus playing the whole piece? Do they set specific goals and targets for themselves? Do they think they can over-rehearse, and how do they know when to stop? How do they go about memorizing a piece? Do they deliberately vary the tempo, stress or mood as they are playing – and if so, why? Do they record themselves playing, and how do they use the recording? Do they rehearse mentally, in their mind's ear and eye, as well as physically? Does it help to imagine the concert hall and the audience as they are practising? What is the balance between practising alone and with their ensemble or orchestra? And so on.

Learning to be a good cellist is very much a matter of learning to learn how to be a good cellist. Everyone now knows that innate talent counts for less than we thought, and that it takes around 10,000 hours of quality practice to get good at a whole lot of things.[7] But what 'quality' means – the intricacies of the craft of practising itself – is still not taught as widely as it might be. There are, of course, big differences in the ways people practise, depending on what their field is, how good they are, and on a host of personal preferences; but there is much that can be taught, and teaching it helps. Knowing how to extract the most learning juice from an hour's practice is a big part of practical intelligence.[8]

> **"**Everyone now knows that innate talent counts for less than we thought, and that it takes around 10,000 hours of quality practice to get good at a whole lot of things.**"**

> **"**Knowing how to extract the most learning juice from an hour's practice is a big part of practical intelligence.**"**

To become a good glass-blower, hockey player, blues singer or cardiologist, you have to have realistic expectations about what the learning journey is going to be like. Beyond learning how to be a good learner, it helps to understand that expertise becomes progressively more intuitive. We will explore intuitive intelligence more in the next chapter, but it is worth noting here that, to progress beyond a certain point, you have to give up thinking about what you are doing, or being able to explain and justify it. That is as true for an expert electrician as it is for the cellist. True experts don't think much about what they are doing; 95 per cent of the time their hands (or feet in the case of some sports) just naturally do the right thing. And they know when and how to think most effectively, and most sparingly.[9]

Overall, there is a wealth of practical knowledge about how to be a more effective learner in the context particularly of sports and music. As we have said, some of this is obviously domain-specific, especially as you progress to higher levels of expertise. But developing mental toughness (resilience and determination), curiosity and questioning, or expanding the ability to use mental rehearsal, is useful for a student chef, designer or nurse, as well as for learning maths or science. Many schools and colleges do not yet teach 'the craft of intelligent learning' as well as they might.

Giving the mind a hand

Seymour Papert co-founded the world-famous Robotics Lab at MIT, and invented Logo, a simple but powerful programming language for children. Early in his career, he worked in a maths classroom in a Junior High School in Massachusetts, and every day he had to walk past the art room to get there. The students were carving sculptures out of blocks of soap. They worked on them for weeks. Papert was fascinated (and challenged) to observe a depth of engagement, thoughtfulness, creativity and collaboration that he had never seen in maths.

He came to see that a big part of the difference lay in working with their hands to craft something 'real' that they could think and talk about as it developed. The students were not just 'mindlessly' whittling away at the soap; they were highly present, using the full learning orchestra playing together. They were looking carefully and feeling with their fingers; experimenting and tinkering as they went along; imagining and wondering about new possibilities; and being thoughtful and self-critical too. To call what they were doing merely 'manual work' was to miss the richness and complexity – the cognitive sophistication – of the learning they were doing.

Papert saw that Jean Piaget, his old mentor, had got it wrong. As children grew up, they did not move from physical learning through imaginary learning and on to formal or rational learning, leaving the earlier modes behind as they 'outgrew' them. On the contrary, imagining and reasoning *added to* observing and experimenting, making practical learning more and more intricate and powerful. Children were not moving through stages in a linear way; they were developing a richer and deeper repertoire of learning instruments that could all play together, making not a series of learning solos but a jazz orchestra of harmonies and interactions. That's what those students were learning in the art room, and to Papert the learning experience in maths came to look rather thin beside it. He resolved – very successfully – to find ways to make learning in maths as rich and 'hands on' as it was in the art room down the corridor.[10]

In real life, people 'think with their hands' as well as with their minds. In fact, hands play an important role in the most advanced forms of human creative thinking.

> **"**Papert saw that Jean Piaget, his old mentor, had got it wrong . . . Children were not moving through stages in a linear way; they were developing a richer and deeper repertoire of learning instruments that could all play together, making not a series of learning solos but a jazz orchestra of harmonies and interactions.**"**

There is now evidence that when people gesture as they are talking, their hands are actually involved, not just in adding emphasis to what it being expressed, but in helping to shape and support the thinking process itself. People gesture more when they are trying to explain difficult things, and when they are 'thinking aloud', than when they are merely describing a solution they have already figured out. When children are asked to explain the thinking behind their answer to a maths question, for example, they are handicapped – literally – if they are required to sit on their hands. Gesturing reflects the close connection between thinking and making – even when the only physical thing you have to make are shapes in the air! (Doodling also helps people attend, think and remember, for the same reason.[11])

And gestures often give evidence of greater understanding than people's tongues do. Researchers Susan Goldin-Meadow and Susan Wagner have found that gesturing adds to creativity. They say:

> 'Gestures can allow people to introduce novel ideas [that are] not entirely consistent with their current beliefs ... without inviting challenge from their own self-monitoring systems ... Once in, those new ideas could catalyze change.'[12] It is as if our hands are connected up to bits of the brain that may 'know' or suspect or wonder about things that our more conscious and deliberate minds are as yet unaware of, or are too inconvenient to currently entertain.

"It is as if our hands are connected up to bits of the brain that may 'know' or suspect or wonder about things that our more conscious and deliberate minds are as yet unaware of, or are too inconvenient to currently entertain."

Indeed, evolutionary psychologists now think that all our skills of thinking actually grew out of our burgeoning ability to use physical tools. Our brains evolved to think with their hands long before they perfected the art of inner speech and logical reasoning. It looks as if our ancestors 'began language-like communication through a kind of sign language, then started augmenting it with vocalizations, and then, as our vocal tracts became more sophisticated, eventually supplanted the gestures like a cast-off scaffold'.[13] But not supplanted it entirely, for the hands continue to play an important role. And you can still see vestiges of that order of priority in the human brain. The area of the brain that controls mathematical reasoning still has strong connections to the area that controls the fingers. It is no accident that the word 'digital' refers both to sophisticated computing and to the bodily appendages that tap the keys on the keyboard.

The intelligence of emotion

The third aspect of physical intelligence we want to mention is emotion. In the old, narrow view of intelligence, emotion was a nuisance. It added personal, untrustworthy interference to the dispassionate workings of reason. Certainly, people's desires and fears steer their thinking all the time, and sometimes for the worse. It is essential, sometimes, to be able to 'take yourself out of the equation' and consider 'the good of all'. That is indeed a civilizing force in society. But emotions are not just primitive glitches to thinking that have to be 'managed' or 'controlled' (as some of the 'emotional intelligence' movement seems to see it). Emotions are vital and valuable components of intelligence itself.

> **"Emotions are vital and valuable components of intelligence itself."**

Neurologist Antonio Damasio has shown, in a series of elegant studies,[14] that people lose real-world intelligence when reason and emotion become disconnected from each other. People with a certain kind of damage to their frontal lobes continue to score highly on IQ tests, and to understand and debate complex ideas, but that rational intelligence no longer influences what they actually do. They can *tell* you the smart thing to do, and then go and do the exact opposite – to their own obvious detriment. (You do not need evident brain damage for this effect to occur: newspapers thrive on stories of very talented people who behave recklessly and self-destructively.) Damasio has found that it is the visceral feelings of emotion and intuition that bind our reason to our action, and when that connection is severed, rational and real-world intelligence are likely to shear apart.

Evolution has provided us with some really useful emotional systems that enable us to cope with various kinds of emergencies and disruptions. The most basic is the Distress System that babies use to attract attention and so be rescued when things go wrong. The Fear System gets our bodies ready to run and hide, and our minds focused on the source of danger. The Disgust System detects poisons (literal or psychological) and closes up the senses against them (we 'wrinkle our noses in disgust') or activates reflexes to expel them. The Shame System gets us to respond to our social transgressions and loss of face by making us look 'hangdog' – i.e. no threat – and inviting forgiveness. The Learning System detects sources of strangeness in the world, and/or inadequacy in our own skills, which are judged not too dangerous, and makes us go and investigate and explore, to build up greater familiarity and competence for next time. And so on.[15]

There are some ten of these basic systems, and they are our intelligent friends. The only problem comes when, as a result of previous experience, they fire off too fast or at the wrong time. Then we become over-aggressive, or over-cautious, or reckless in our investigations. Understood rightly, any faults are not in our emotional systems themselves, but in their misfiring: in habits of reacting that served us well once but don't any longer. It would be useful for all children to understand this, and to get interested not in how to 'control' or over-ride their (troublesome) emotional reactions, but how to retune them skilfully, to bring them up to date. Understanding how to retune outdated habits makes a major contribution to real-world intelligence.[16]

> "Understanding how to retune outdated habits makes a major contribution to real-world intelligence."

Starting out

Of late, many people in education have become interested in the physical, bodily side of students' learning. This interest is welcome, and overdue. Sometimes, though, this has taken the form of a search for, or gullibility towards, neuroscientific sound-bites of dubious worth, and quick fixes of various kinds. The possibilities of 'magic bullet' drugs and food supplements that might 'make your child brighter' tend to hit the headlines every so often, but usually fail to survive proper scientific scrutiny. Extravagant claims have been made for the boosting of intelligence by fish oil capsules, for example, that have yet to be properly substantiated.[17]

Teachers have even been told that they must keep their students sipping water – preferably from special hi-tech bottles – or their brains will dry up and learning will suffer. Of course it is useful to be able to take a drink when you are thirsty, but the idea that, after thousands of generations of evolution, the human brain still hasn't figured out how to keep itself damp for an hour, does rather defy belief. And controlled studies have actually discovered that being encouraged to drink water when you are not actively thirsty tends to decrease your 'cognitive performance' rather than boost it.

There are products that claim that doing some tricky gymnastic exercises – touching your right ear to your left knee, and vice versa, as fast as you can – will develop specific bundles of nerve fibres in the brain, and therefore make you smarter, but here again there is much more commercial hype than hard data. But lots of us are susceptible to advice based on 'the latest brain research': studies at Yale have shown that people are more likely to buy a bad explanation for something if it contains some gratuitous references to the brain! Unfortunately, calling something 'Brain Training', rather than just a Computer Game, does not seem to ensure that it will make you smarter in any other context than that of playing the game.[18]

Management guru Stephen Covey[19] has a really useful idea which can easily be adapted for the classroom: the pause button.

A useful tool: the pause button

This is a simple but effective routine for children (and adults!) to use when their feelings run away with them.

Think of the pause button on a CD, DVD or MP3 player to get the idea. (Pressing it freezes the action for a moment until you unpress it.) Then move from metaphor to the reality of a classroom, corridor or school playground situation to see how it can be taught and applied.

Students learn that when they feel their feelings running away from them they can 'press their pause button' and buy a valuable few moments to consider whether the course of action they have unwittingly embarked upon is a smart one or not.

There are many classroom management techniques – 'time out' and 'spending time in the quiet corner' are good examples – that effectively use this approach.

Going deeper

However flawed the rationale, recognizing that young people have active and energetic bodies, as well as minds, must be a good thing; and allowing them to let off some physical steam every now and then, and to drink when they are thirsty, has to be a start. The deeper implications of embodied cognition, though, are only just beginning to be explored.

Some schools are starting to realize what Seymour Papert noticed: that many young people's learning energies are engaged more deeply, and their minds are therefore being stretched and expanded more powerfully, when they are working over time to shape and craft physical material, than when they are working only with listening, reading and writing. In so-called 'forest schools',[20] for example, where children work and learn together in natural surroundings, teachers are often astonished at how attentive, determined and thoughtful (in both senses of that word) young people

> 66 Many young people's learning energies are engaged more deeply, and their minds are therefore being stretched and expanded more powerfully, when they are working over time to shape and craft physical material, than when they are working only with listening, reading and writing. 99

turn out to be. A student of Guy's, Elizabeth Cooper, found in her masters' dissertation that a group of youngsters with 'moderate learning difficulties' literally turned into different, more intelligent, people in the woods. Not only their habits but also their self-images changed significantly. And while Bill was the Director of *Learning through Landscapes*, a not-for-profit organization extolling practical, experiential learning, he regularly saw telling examples of just how differently students used their minds and bodies when learning outside.[21]

But practical, embodied learning is not just for those who are struggling with school. There are many stories of high achieving scientists, surgeons, architects and designers – even philosophers and barristers – who developed their lifelong habits of curiosity and resilience through tinkering and crafting with their hands. Practical learning is not just for those who are not 'bright enough' to take the academic route. It should be part of every student's learning diet. In the light of our new understanding of the close links between body, brain and mind, the very opposition between 'practical' and 'academic' is outmoded and dysfunctional. The old image of the Oxbridge or Ivy League 'hero' who gets a first *and* rows in the Boat Race or plays league basketball need to be replaced with a more sophisticated sense of how mind and body work together.

> "In the light of our new understanding of the close links between body, brain and mind, the very opposition between 'practical' and 'academic' is outmoded and dysfunctional."

Gerver Tulley is the founder of a summer school for young people in Montara, California, called the Tinkering School.[22] He cheerfully reassures parents that, yes, probably their child will come home with some scrapes and bruises, but they will have learned how to build a gravity-powered wooden roller-coaster with their hands – and in the process, will have developed their all-round cognitive capacity. Tulley has a TED talk on the web called 'Five dangerous things you should let your kids do'[23] that is worth a look. The dangerous things include playing with fire, learning to use a pen-knife, making and learning to throw a spear, driving a car (not on the highway, obviously), and taking things to bits. He thinks that learning to be 'manipulate', as well as articulate, is the foundation for real-world intelligence.

> **"Learning to be 'manipulate', as well as articulate, is the foundation for real-world intelligence."**
>
> adapted from Gerver Tulley

Learning to think while you are making things with your hands is not a nostalgic throw-back to a pre-digital world. The father of one of Tulley's tinkering students was a vice-president at Adobe, the giant software developer, and now Tulley teaches his tinkering skills to front-rank software designers at Adobe, and that experience informs how they work. Stanford University introduced hands-on courses when the professors of engineering, architecture and design realized that many of their students had never built a model airplane or taken a bike apart – and it showed in their thinking. And at the Massachusetts Institute of Technology – Seymour Papert's university – course MAS.863 is regularly over-subscribed: it is called 'How to Make (Almost) Anything', and it teaches some of the brightest students in the USA how to use a variety of physical tools. It would be great if that deep coalition of the physical and the cognitive were to inform the curriculum in more schools – secondary in particular.

Ideas into practice

Unless you are in a Montessori or Forest School where learning through practical experience is the norm, it may be that you are feeling starved of this kind of approach. To help you think how to try out ideas about practical intelligence, you might like to wonder:

1 What is my experience of the relative esteem of practical and academic learning? What were the implicit messages of my own schooling, and are they different from the setting in which I work now?

2 Is there more I could do to help learners develop their ability (and inclination) to practise more effectively? Could I help students understand that every time they write, they are not just 'doing it' well or badly, but practising and experimenting with their writing?

3 How could I create more opportunities for the kind of engagement that Seymour Papert noticed? Do I have any leeway to create longer-term learning projects in which students can really get their teeth into some real challenges?

4 Could I tell my students about the 'pause button', and do I think it would help them to learn and practise more effectively? Would it help me?

5 Could I use the school grounds more effectively to create opportunities for experiential learning? Are there more things that the students could physically make and do that would help the school as a whole?

6 Am I being adventurous enough in what I offer my students? Are there things I could let them do that would build their physical strength and skill, as well as their responsibility?

7 Which subjects might particularly benefit from more practical learning? Could I explore with colleagues the potential of Science and History to develop the dispositions of tinkering and re-drafting – as well as Physical Education and Design Technology?

4

Intelligence is Intuitive

We know much more than we know we know.

Michael Polanyi[1]

Boy looking out of classroom window.

TEACHER: 'What are you doing, boy?'
BOY: 'Thinking, sir.'
TEACHER: 'Well stop it!'

Imagine you are house-hunting. You've got all the brochures and met all the agents, and now you've whittled it down to four possibilities. But it's a tough choice. There are so many different factors, it's hard to know how to weight them against each other. One is cheaper but it would need a fair bit doing to it to make it nice. Another is close to the train station, but the local school does not have such a good reputation. The third has a lovely garden but looks onto a rather ugly block of flats. The fourth has the third bedroom that would be useful as a study, but there was loud music coming from next door when you called round. And so on. You sit down to weigh up all the information you have, and then decide which one to go for. How best to go about making that decision? Dutch psychologist Ap Dijksterhuis has investigated this question in detail, and he has found that the more you try to be rational, the less good your decision. That's right: in situations like this, the attempt to be as methodical and explicit as you can is actually counter-productive. The most rational decision-makers tend to zoom in on a smaller number of considerations, and to pay less attention to the more complex bigger picture.[2]

In another study in the USA, students at the end of their first year at college were investigated as they were considering which psychology courses to select for the next semester. They were given full details of the courses, including comments from other students who had taken the courses the previous year. Some of the students were asked to think as carefully as they could, so that they would be able to explain and justify their intentions. Others were invited to make up their minds on a more intuitive basis. When all the students were followed up the next year, the intuitive group were more likely to be satisfied with their choices, and less likely to have changed their minds, than those who had been encouraged to be more explicit about their reasons.[3]

Getting to grips with intuitive intelligence

These findings are quite challenging to the conventional view of intelligence. That view highly values abstract, rational, explicit, conscious thinking and decision-making, and is rather scornful of any kind of thinking that doesn't measure up to those strict criteria. If you can't offer a logical rationale, or fail to 'show your workings', the general assumption is that your thinking is sloppy, and likely to be worse. Intuitive thinking was in general seen as lazy and less intelligent, typical of the young, the uneducated, and often of women. Stereotypically, it was the educated adult male who was able to think in the clearest, most dispassionate, and therefore most intelligent, way, and it was his job, therefore, to apply his high intelligence to making the most important decisions.[4]

So is rational intelligence now debunked by science? Should we throw away our list of pros and cons and now simply rely on our gut feelings? Well, no. But the situation is certainly more complicated than the High Rationalists would have us believe. Reason and intuition turn out to be complementary ways of being intelligent, and if we are to educate children to be the smartest they can be, we need to balance the two, and help them to understand when and how they work best together. They need to know about the limitations of 'giving reasons' and 'showing your workings', as well as the strengths. They need to know when and how to listen to their intuitions, and what weight to give to them.

> "Reason and intuition turn out to be complementary ways of being intelligent, and if we are to educate children to be the smartest they can be, we need to balance the two, and help them to understand when and how they work best together."

The elastic brain

As we saw earlier, now we know a little more about the brain we are able to expand our model of intelligence to include ways of knowing and learning that are not as conscious, rational and explicit. Neuro-scientists often imagine the brain as a mountainous landscape comprising a vast range of bowls connected by a network of valleys. These patterns represent concepts and habits that have been eroded and established by experience, so that neural activation, as it flows around, tends to follow the worn-away channels. These channels and dips act as 'attractors' of this activity, so that new patterns of stimulation that fall on the landscape are likely to be funnelled into the existing pathways. Features and ideas that have occurred frequently together tend to be bound together by well-worked channels, so that activity in one is likely to flow into and activate the other.

Provided you remember that this metaphorical landscape represents the *functional* 'closeness' of ideas to each other, which is not at all the same thing as physical proximity in the actual brain, this is not a bad image. In reality, the concept *cat*, for example, which comprises a tightly interconnected bundle of sounds, visual images, touch, reactions, feelings and memories, will be spread out across the whole brain, so when you are thinking about your childhood cat, or hear a miaow outside the door, what happens in the brain is more like switching on a large circuit of fairy-lights across the brain than a big bulb in a single location.

But what neuroscientists have found out requires us to complicate this pastoral image. For the landscape is not solid and stable, but highly elastic – more Bouncy Castle (Jolly Jumps or Moonbounces in the US) than alpine scenery. So although experience does wear long-term channels into the neural landscape, its steepness is continually being modified by the coming and going of much more short-term changes in moods, priorities and

> **"Although experience does wear long-term channels into the neural landscape, its steepness is continually being modified by the coming and going of much more short-term changes in moods, priorities and expectations."**

expectations. That is one of the jobs of our big frontal lobes: to modulate the cragginess of different bits of the landscape. So if you are thirsty, your elastic landscape in the area of *drinks* dips so that you are primed to notice taps and vending machines, and activity is more likely to flow in that direction. If you are scared of spiders, the *spider* terrain will be permanently sharpened and lowered, so that you will automatically notice the stalk from the top of a tomato that someone dropped on the kitchen floor, and attend to it carefully to make sure it isn't a spider.

More generally, the frontal lobes can set the landscape to be more mountainous or more flat, and can also vary whether there can be a number of centres that are active at the same time, or whether there can only be one, a single 'train of thought'. (The brain has some very clever ways of controlling itself like this, so there can be several dimly-lit patterns active at once, or alternatively there is a 'winner-takes-all' situation in which the strongest pattern at any moment automatically inhibits all its competitors.) Roughly, the more mountainous the brain, the more your trains of thought are likely to be clear-cut, conscious and unambiguous; to follow the most well-worn and familiar grooves; and to travel fast. You respond to situations in a focused, confident and conventional manner. You don't bother with the fine print and ignore any minor incongruities. But if your brain sets itself flatter, into what we might call Meadow mode (or more technically, a lower state of cortical arousal) you are more likely to see the shades of grey and be aware of multiple possibilities. You stay closer to the details of experience, rather than looking through the spectacles of your familiar habits and constructs. When you are trying to 'stay on track', have a clear idea of what your priorities are, and want to be clear, fast and efficient, you are in Mountain mode. When you are more open, playful and dreamy, you are in Meadow mode (and, of course, you can be anywhere in between; it's a matter of degree).[5]

Obviously, both are useful. Mountain mode works well in routine situations, and helps you be focused and disciplined in your thinking and analysing. But it can only handle a small number of variables at once. It sacrifices scope for precision, and creativity for efficiency. Meadow mode is more leisurely and creative. Because more patterns can be active at once, the brain increases its chances of finding a new pattern that might connect them up in an original way. Because the land is flat, neural patterns are much more able to bleed into one another, so you can find connections that are less stereotyped or conventional. But if you *stay* in Meadow mode, you may never harness your creative musings and turn them into something useful. To do that, you'll need to sharpen up, concentrate and be more disciplined.

So the intelligent mind is fluid and elastic. It has access to both Mountain and Meadow modes, and is able to segue between them. Indeed, electroencephalogram (EEG) studies of genuinely creative people show that they have the knack of doing exactly that. If you ask them to dream up a story, and then to work on improving it, you can see their brains flipping between the two modes. They can 'go meadow', in order to allow their brains to bubble up with some interesting possibilities. And then they can switch into 'mountain' in order to analyse, evaluate and improve. Less creative types tend to get stuck in one mode or the other, and are not able to get the benefit of both. In one of Colin Martindale's studies[6] in this area, most of the less creative people turned out to be stuck in Mountain mode. They were only able to try to *think* up the story; they didn't know how to get their brains to *dream* it up for them. If you are thinking this sounds reminiscent of the 'left brain, right brain' idea, you are half right (!). There are suggestions that – in normally right-handed people – the default setting of the left hemisphere is more mountainous, and of the right hemisphere more meadowy, thus allowing them to have the best of both worlds – at the same time.

What is happening in the decision-making experiments with which we started this chapter is that people are being told to switch into Mountain mode, when the task they are facing is actually one that benefits from a more meadowy attitude. Mountain mode works well when there are only a few variables at play, which need to be tracked carefully and related to each other precisely. As situations get more complex, and the number of considerations begins to exceed the number that Mountain mode can handle, so it become preferable to shift to a more diffused way of thinking that allows more factors to be taken into account simultaneously, but at a lower level of awareness. That is the intuitive way.

In Meadow mode, the brain is better able to keep a running tally of a greater number of variables and so, although you cannot explain or justify it, your 'feeling' about which house or course to go for is likely to be more trustworthy (provided you have been paying attention to all the information). If you are made to stick with Mountain mode, you are like a three-ball juggler who is being tossed more and more balls. In order to keep juggling, you have to keep making split-second decisions about which ones to drop. Strict rationality requires you to neglect information that exceeds its capacity, to the detriment of your intelligence. That is why very clever people like lawyers sometimes make astoundingly 'stupid' decisions; they have created water-tight arguments, but only by neglecting some of the less-easy-to-articulate, but nevertheless very important, considerations. This is what people mean, in everyday language, when they accuse highly-educated people of not having much 'common sense'.

In Mountain mode, the brain is more rigid and more literal in its way of functioning. It is less likely to see the funny side, because humour often relies on being open to the absurd, and to rapidly switching frames of reference in order to 'get the joke'. It is not surprising, therefore, that showing people a clip of *Fawlty Towers* (choose your own favourite comedy show if this does not do it for you!), or giving them a quick relaxation exercise, increases their subsequent creativity. Meetings are likely to be more productive, and lessons more interesting, if they start with a joke or a building of rapport that puts people into the right frame of mind to be receptive to new ideas and more creative in their response.[7]

Getting less deliberate

Intelligence is also increased though incubation – periods when you stop thinking deliberately about the problem and allow your brain to drift into more relaxing areas. In one version of Dijksterhuis's experiments on house-buying, he varied the time people had to make their decision. One group made their decision straight after having reviewed all the information. Two other groups had to wait for a quarter of an hour before deciding. One of those groups was urged to review the information carefully. The other was prevented from doing so by being given mental arithmetic tasks to fill the time. When Dijksterhuis compared the quality of the decisions taken by the three groups, he found that the ones who had the delay, but were prevented from conscious thought, outperformed the other two. And the group who thought carefully for 15 minutes did no better than those who made their choice immediately.

Research on incubation suggests at least two reasons why it works. The first is straightforward. When you are straining for a result, it is all too easy to get locked into a way of looking at the problem that stops you seeing the solution. A break – or a period of sleep, especially – allows the brain to reset itself, so that when you come back to the problem, you don't have the same set of blinkers on.

The second reason is more intuitive. When you work hard on a problem without success, your brain effectively creates a 'black hole', so to speak, to represent what the kind of shape a satisfying solution would have. And this representation is primed, so it exerts (as black holes do) a sort of magnetic attraction on what is happening in a wide vicinity of functional brain space around it. When you take a break from your hard thinking, this background 'pull' remains, so that any stray thought that bears even the slightest relationship to the problem gets attracted, and might – just might – provide a fruitful metaphor or snippet of information that could be the key. Of course many such associations turn out to be useless. You don't notice them. But occasionally something fires up a new thought, one that immediately attracts your conscious attention, and enables you to have a 'brainwave'.

It is not just artistic 'types' who know how to make good use of this kind of intuition. In a survey of Nobel science laureates, more than 90 per cent said their intuition had been invaluable. Konrad Lorenz, who won the prize for medicine in 1973, for example, explained how he capitalized on this rhythm between hard work and incubation:

This apparatus which intuits has to have an enormous basis of known facts at its disposal with which to play. And it plays in a very mysterious manner, because . . . it sort of keeps all known facts afloat, waiting for them to fall into place, like a jigsaw puzzle. And if you press . . . if you try to permutate your knowledge, nothing comes of it. You must give a sort of mysterious pressure, and then rest, and suddenly BING!, the solution comes.[8]

Rita Levi-Montalcini, Nobel laureate in 1986, said something similar:

> **You've been thinking about something without willing to for a long time . . . Then, all of a sudden, the problem is opened to you in a flash, and you suddenly see the answer.**
>
> Rita Levi-Montalcini

You've been thinking about something without willing to for a long time . . . Then, all of a sudden, the problem is opened to you in a flash, and you suddenly see the answer.[9]

Notice that these insights do not come out of nowhere. You cannot just lie on your back, gaze at the ceiling, and have a Nobel-prize-winning idea float into your mind. The creative intuition comes to a mind that is well stocked with information and experience, and which has been trying to make sense of it all for a long time. Intuition complements the hard work of thinking, information gathering and experimenting; it does not obviate it.

> **Creative intuition comes to a mind that is well stocked with information and experience, and which has been trying to make sense of it all for a long time. Intuition complements the hard work of thinking, information gathering and experimenting; it does not obviate it.**

Some insights, like the two examples just given, are remarkable because they come with such abrupt clarity. But not all intuitions arrive in such style. Many are more gentle and hesitant, offering a glimmer of a possibility, rather than the certainty of a breakthrough. The English language has nice words for these more delicate intuitions: we call them hunches, inklings, promptings and feelings. And they make themselves known in a variety of ways. Some come as clear mental pictures, but many are more hazy. Albert Einstein said that his 'working language of thought' was not symbols and equations but an array of 'more or less clear images',[10] many of which were more like physical promptings than mental pictures.

Some intuitions definitely come as physical sensations or even movements. 'By the pricking of my thumbs, something evil this way comes', said one of the witches in *Macbeth*. Stories and films can 'make your flesh creep', or 'the hairs on the back of your neck stand up'. You can understand something deeply without being able to put your finger on it, as when you are 'touched' or 'moved' by a piece of music or a scene in a play. And, as we saw in an earlier chapter, children can give evidence of their understanding – of mathematical concepts, for example – through their gestures, even before their more cautious rational minds are able to articulate or explain that understanding. This 'leakage' of knowing or understanding through physical or sensory intuitions, before the brain is ready to speak more directly, as it were, has been established by experiment. As they work through a problem, what people think are irrational hunches or even pure guesses reveal, on close analysis, the gradual development of pre-conscious insight.[11]

> **"What people think are irrational hunches or even pure guesses reveal, on close analysis, the gradual development of pre-conscious insight."**
> adapted from Bowers et al.

As intuition expert Eugene Sadler-Smith puts it, 'Everyone has intuition. It is one of the hallmarks of how human beings think and behave. It's impossible for us to function effectively without using gut feeling.'[12] And schools need to wise up to how they can harness the power of intuitive ways of knowing things.

Starting out

Having access to this twilight zone of the mind, understanding its benefits and being able to harness them, and knowing how to relate it to more conscious and focused kinds of thinking, all make you smarter. So how can educators make use of this information in order to help children and young people become more intelligent?

Some primary schools occasionally involve children in extended periods of this kind of 'manic creativity', in which, for a few days, the normal curriculum is temporarily replaced by a frenzy of arts-based activity – composing, rehearsing, painting and cutting out – that culminates in an enthusiastically-received presentation to parents and others of a 'Victorian classroom' or a 'mediaeval fair'. The children are usually highly engaged and, indeed, creative. Teachers make sure that the quieter ones do not get excluded and make a contribution of which they can be proud. But it is not clear that these sporadic events create any lasting change in the way children go about thinking in less dramatic contexts.

There are also doubts about the effectiveness of techniques such as brainstorming. The rationale for encouraging an uncritical flow of ideas emphasizes building confidence and creating a more intuitive state of flow. But while one can sympathize with the thinking behind such techniques, it turns out that they rarely generate seriously useful ideas. Some people have a lot of fun letting their imaginations run away with them, but the ideas produced in this kind of situation are often shallow and unproductive.

Research has uncovered a number of problems. First, the ideas that come immediately, 'off the top of your head', tend not to be the ones that are the most productive. More thoughtful ideas that turn out to have greater potential often come later, after that first 'dump'. Yet a lot of brainstorming stops before thinking gets to that stage. Second, it turns out to be harder for people to switch off their critical minds than this model assumes. Some people still hold back because of 'evaluation apprehension': they worry that their ideas will eventually attract negative comment. And, third, there is a problem summed up in those two words 'some people'. Brainstorming tends to get dominated by extroverts, and by people who don't mind 'shooting their mouth off', and allows others to indulge in a bit of what psychologists have dubbed 'social loafing'. The less confident or the less pushy contribute less, and the intense clamour of brainstorming militates against their ideas getting into the pool that is subsequently considered.

These studies have enabled some teachers (and business managers) to devise more productive alternatives; ones that preserve the strengths of brainstorming but improve the quality of ideas that are generated. One method, devised by business psychologist Peter Heslin, is called brainwriting.[13] Students work in groups of four. Once the original problem or challenge has been set, the first ten-minute period involves everyone *in silence* writing down some ideas on slips of paper. The group members look at each other's slips of paper and may add some further ideas of their own. Each person uses a different coloured pen so their contributions can be identified. When a slip has four ideas on it, it is placed in the centre of the table for all to see. When there are a good number of such slips, the process moves into the second stage. Each student goes off on their own and attempts to write down as many of the ideas as they can remember. They know they are going to have to do this during the first stage, so they are set to pay careful attention to each other's contributions. Then they move into the third stage, in which, still working alone, the students attempt to generate more and better ideas. Finally, they share and discuss. In a preliminary study, Heslin found that this technique significantly improved the number and quality of students' creative ideas, relative to the more familiar kind of brainstorming, or to students simply working on their own.

Going deeper

Many teachers are now exploring ways of getting students to practise interweaving 'mountain' and 'meadow' modes in their learning. It could be as simple as increasing the amount of time that they give students to think, after they have asked a question (instead of taking the first 'hands up' right answer and moving swiftly along). This is a technique adopted by 'Assessment for Learning' to create greater engagement, though we don't know if it increases the *quality* of thinking and learning. Other teachers have set up distinct places in the classroom that encourage children to be aware and make use of different kinds of thinking. As part of an action research project, Vicky Scale-Constantinou, a Year 1 teacher at Roath Park Primary School in Cardiff, discovered that 'none of the children saw imagination or creativity as a significant aspect of [their normal] learning'.[14] So she modified the use of space, resources and language in her classroom to try to change that.

With the aid of a black sheet she transformed the 'home corner' into a 'creative corner': a quiet tent with some dim lights and music playing inside. The children were encouraged to make use of the creative corner when they wanted to use their imaginations.

Whole-class imagination sessions were also held in which they got used to closing their eyes and letting ideas 'bubble up' into their minds. The children decided they would like to record their imaginings so each designed their own 'imagination book', and time was regularly found to use them. Importantly, says Vicky, 'I made it clear to the children that I would not mark these books and that the content was their choice.' Each child also made their own 'imagination badge' that they were entitled to wear whenever they felt they had used their imagination in their day-to-day work. And talking about the value of imagination in learning became a routine part of the classroom environment.

Individual interviews were conducted with all the children both before and after these changes were implemented. These revealed an increase in the number of children who said they regularly used their imaginations (from 16 to 22), and a very significant increase in those who said they made use of their imagination to help them learn (from 4 to 19). Asked to elaborate on the latter, typical comments from the children included: 'Sometimes when I need help I don't need it because I use my imagination', 'It gives you ideas because it gives you a chance to think more', and 'It makes my sentences more exciting'. Vicky was surprised to discover that a high proportion of the 'middle-ability' boys in the class had responded particularly well: 'they were the pupils who seemed to value the use of imagination most and articulated it best'. There is evidence that the development of the *disposition* to make use of imagination in the course of routine learning had been strengthened, and that it had become second nature to many of the children. 'Quite a few of the children now ask to go into the creative corner if they are stuck in their work, or if they feel they want to improve their work.'

An example of how to work on building creative capacity with older students is provided by Mary Larrabee, a Year 9 teacher in the USA. She has used an approach to creative thinking and writing called 'Thinking at the Edge' (TATE) developed by the renowned philosopher Eugene Gendlin.[15] According to Gendlin, TATE 'is a systematic way to articulate in new terms something which needs to be said, but is at first only an inchoate bodily sense'; in other words, it tries to teach students how to articulate their intuitive ideas – without losing their freshness and originality. One of Gendlin's undergraduate students called it a way of working with things 'about which we have to do hemming and hawing'. TATE is a systematic way of attending to these bodily intuitions, and trying to put them into written form with the help of a partner, who acts as kind of secretary-cum-counsellor, transcribing your 'hemming and hawing' and helping you to find connections and better ways to phrase what you want to say (but not trying to criticize or improve the ideas themselves).

Students in Larrabee's class were asked to think of an area of their life that was significant but puzzling to them, and to identify any hazy images or feelings that went along with that puzzle. With the help of their 'scribe', they were asked to develop something in writing that captured a new understanding, and which they subsequently shared with family and friends. Though there is as yet little in the way of hard evaluation of TATE, Larrabee claims some success, and quotes some of the students' reactions to the process. Their descriptions of the intuitive senses on which they were trying to focus were revealing, and sometimes rather creative in their own right:

It's a big black bubble type of thing ... and little smokes wafting out that you can catch, something that feels original, coming out of my innermost being.

You go blank and stop thinking and find something . . . like waking-up – this is where your mind's supposed to start thinking.

A place inside . . . [where you can] just be yourself and release whatever thoughts and be what you are.

Commenting on the whole process, another student said:

The best part – being able to express yourself, thinking outside of what I would normally think about – it led me to find myself.

TATE is as yet a new and relatively untried approach to the cultivation of intuitive intelligence, but early reports suggest that both young people and adults find the process interesting and even exciting. The idea that it sometimes takes intelligent people time to find the words to say what they want to say can be liberating. The idea that knowing how to make this time, and to use it skilfully, are aspects of intelligence itself, and can help to undercut the pernicious idea that clever people are always fast, and that 'slow' is an acceptable euphemism for 'stupid'. Robert Sternberg has argued that: 'If anything, the essence of intelligence would seem to be in knowing when to think and act quickly and knowing when to think and act slowly.'[16]

> **The essence of intelligence would seem to be in knowing when to think and act quickly and knowing when to think and act slowly.**
>
> Robert Sternberg

Elsewhere[17] we have written about ways of developing states of mind which are conducive to the flourishing of imagination and intuition and now we offer a tool for you to try with yourself, with colleagues or with students based on a process which we have used in other contexts. Although the experience may be unfamiliar to you, once you have tried it a few times you should find that it helps to get you ready to think freshly, and to allow new possibilities to bubble up into your mind!

A useful tool: don't know mind

Here's a simple meditation that you might like to use yourself or with students to create a more relaxed state of mind, one in which your intuition may flourish! You may need to get someone to read it out to you, or make your own recording.

Sit in a comfortable chair, fairly upright, with hands resting on your lap. Close your eyes and take three slow deep breaths, allowing yourself to make an audible sigh as you do so. Sit quietly for a moment simply listening to the sounds around you but trying not to focus on any one particular sound. Just enjoy listening to the noises around you.

Now breathe in slowly until your lungs are comfortably full. Hold the breath for a moment and then let it out in a slow steady stream of air. Wait for a second or two and then start to breathe regularly in a nice slow regular rhythm.

Now on each in-breath, say to yourself 'Clear mind; clear mind; clear mind.' Repeat the phrase 'clear mind' slowly two or three times on each in-breath so it fills up the time the breath takes.

Then on the out-breath say to yourself 'Don't know'. Draw out the 'don't' and the 'know' so that they fill the time the out-breath takes. Imagine your mind is letting go of everything it knows so that when you get to the end of the out-breath your mind is alert and open but still and empty.

Ideas into practice

Many of the decisions we take in a typical day at school are likely to involve intuition. Yet, as a legitimate way of knowing and being, intuition is almost invisible in most school curricula. To help you think how you might try out ideas about intuitive intelligence, you might like to wonder:

1 How much of what I do is based on intuition? How could I notice more about the relationship between my deliberate thinking and my intuition? When does thinking help me do a better job, and are there times when it actually gets in the way?

2 What do my students understand by the idea of intuition? Could I talk to them more about intuitive intelligence, and when it is good – or bad – to think about what they are doing?

3 Can I create more situations in which my students' intuition can flourish? Does intuition only really work reliably in areas where people have much more experience than most students have?

4 Could my colleagues and I get together somehow to plan lessons that cultivate intelligent intuitive thinking more effectively?

5 Could we weave intuitive thinking into subjects where it doesn't normally get noticed, like maths and science?

6 How could I encourage students to use intuitive thinking in their homework?

7 Could I create an environment like the one Vicky Scale-Constantinou developed, where students can learn how to make use of the more dreamy sides of their minds?

5

Intelligence is Distributed

In the world outside school, part of knowing how to learn and solve complex problems involves knowing how to . . . deftly use the features of the physical and media environment . . . A central goal for an empowering education [therefore] is to nurture the learners' attitudes and talents in designing distributed intelligence . . . We should reorient the educational emphasis from individual, tool-free cognition to facilitating individuals' responsive and novel uses of resources for creative and intelligent activity alone and in collaboration.

Roy Pea[1]

People are smart in large measure because they have invented, and make good use of, smart tools. We use our intelligence to figure things out, and then we build tools that embody this intelligence, so we don't have to do it all over again, every time we want to achieve the same goal.

For example, every year a forest ranger has to calculate the amount of lumber there is in a piece of woodland. Her trees grow straight and tall, so the volume of wood in a tree is near-enough the cross-sectional area times the height. To find the area, she first wraps a conventional tape-measure round the tree

> "People are smart in large measure because they have invented, and make good use of, smart tools."

to get the length of the circumference, and then, using her high-school geometry, she calculates the diameter of the tree, and then uses that to calculate the area. If she has to do this for every tree, it is a very cumbersome process, and she is likely to make mistakes. So, using her maths, she figures out the formula that relates the area directly to the circumference (Area = Circumference squared divided by 4 x pi, if you want to check it), and then – here's the clever bit – makes herself a new tape measure that reads off the area directly. Using this, her task is a lot simpler, and she doesn't make nearly so many mistakes. This is what human beings do all the time, and the collective intelligence of our societies depends on this vast collection of smart tools that augment our own intelligence.[2]

Some intelligence-augmenting tools are rather more hi-tech, and they are being invented every day. Here is a more futuristic example. Imagine that you are walking down the street wearing your memospecs. It is 2015, not so far into the future, and you are trying out a new bit of kit. Attached to the spectacles is a small camera that is in wireless communication with a computer. The computer contains face recognition software, and a database of your friends and acquaintances, with useful information about their children's names, the meal you had the last time you met, and so on. When the camera/computer detects a face it knows, some of this information is fed back to you and displayed on the 'autocue' built into the spectacles, which function both as vision-correctors and as a monitor for the retrieved data. So, despite your own fallible memory for people, you can now confidently walk up to your acquaintance and ask after Monica and little Zak, and reminisce about those fabulous lobsters you shared at the conference in San Francisco seven years ago. Your social intelligence (see more on this in Chapter 6) is sneakily augmented by technology, brain and computer working seamlessly together to make you a smarter person.[3]

Getting to grips with distributed intelligence

We may well be on the brink of an explosion of this kind of intelligence-enhancing technology. Household robots, wearable software and cognition-enhancing drugs are already a reality, and the prospects are both exciting and disconcerting. However, the augmentation of intelligence through the smart harnessing of external resources is not in itself anything new. The first flint-stones augmented the human ability to sever and tear. The wheel augmented our inherent ability to move – as, later, did the jet engine and the running shoe. The slide-rule augmented our ability to calculate. And the invention of text augmented the pre-existing abilities to communicate and to remember. The way we find, make and use tools to expand our ability to get interesting things done is so amazing, and so ubiquitous, that it has often been proposed as one of the defining characteristics of the human species

> **"The way we find, make and use tools to expand our ability to get interesting things done is so amazing, and so ubiquitous, that it has often been proposed as one of the defining characteristics of the human species."**

(though some other animals do use tools in a rudimentary way as well). *Homo sapiens* is unique in its propensity to create and adopt 'mindware upgrades' of many and various kinds.

The interactions between tools and minds are so intricate that many people – such as the Scottish philosopher Andy Clark, from whom we borrowed the example of the memospecs – are now arguing that it is not actually possible to separate them. Clark suggests, in his provocative book *Natural-Born Cyborgs*,[4] that there is no meaningful difference, now, between breaking your BlackBerry and having a mini-stroke. Both events create the same kind of palpable sense of disability and disorientation. We move so effortlessly and incessantly between the exercise of our on-board memory and reasoning and the memory and reasoning afforded by our PDAs and laptops, and it has become so habitual and natural to do so, that it is quite artificial to try to draw a line between brain and tool, and say that the 'real' intelligence lives only in one rather than the other. Just as a blind person feels the world at the end of her stick, and writers feel the paper at the end of their pencils (and not at the end of their fingers), so we expand our sense of self to include physical intelligence-enhancers of all kinds.[5]

As this chapter is being written, the text on the screen that some fingers typed just a moment ago now feeds back through authorial eyes enabling clarification and development of the message as it appears on the screen. The text and the writer's thinking mind are yoked together in the process of writing, and the text itself is a product that becomes a thinking aid, that gets redrafted and improved, as a result of this interaction, into a better product.

Both of us tend to have papers and books around our computers as we write. In many of these there are scrawled annotations, sometimes from a few years back, that, if we can read them, remind us of illustrations and trains of thought that our brains on their own would not have recalled. In the act of typing the brain reminds its owner (or is it itself?) of something read a few months ago about 'thinkering'. And a quick moment on Google has it up on the screen again, ready to be reincorporated into the writer's mind and then, via fingers, to be reinserted into a document.

The intelligent agent in all this has to be not just the person but 'person-plus': writer plus spectacles plus laptop plus internet plus books plus old annotations plus filing system plus office floor (that allows documents to be visible and easily retrieved at a glance) plus pad of paper plus pen plus plan of book plus drawing pins plus plus plus . . . It would make no sense for someone to deprive a writer of all these prostheses – oh yes, plus dictionary, that has just enabled a quick check whether the word 'prosthesis' can be used in this sense – and then say 'OK, now show me how smart you are as professors'; no more sense than it would to take David Beckham's boots and ball away and ask him to demonstrate his prowess as a footballer.

The role of tools in our lives

It's not just that we come to treat these tools as if they were part of us, and depend upon them. The tools change us. To become a London taxi-driver people use maps to learn their way around, and as they do so, the bit of their brain that stores spatial maps gets bigger. As someone interacts with their piano, the neurons in their motor cortex that control their fingers become more bushy and more precisely interconnected with each other. In order to get the most out of our tools, we have to practise with them, and as we do so we discover more of what they can do, and become more adept at exploiting their potential. The more I hammer, the more I come to think like a hammerer; the more I nurse, the more intricate becomes my notion of a 'patient'.

As technology changes, so people are changed by it. The invention of the fibreglass pole enabled pole-vaulters to raise the world record height by nearly a metre – but they had to learn a difficult new technique to do so. Previous champions who couldn't adapt lost their records (and complained bitterly that the use of the new pole was 'cheating').[6] The invention of the microphone, and the opportunities for amplification and recording that it made possible, made a different style of singing possible too. Where previous band singers had to use a strong tenor voice to be heard above the accompaniment, Bing Crosby discovered that with the microphone he could use a softer baritone and still be heard. The ability to sing more softly allowed the communication of greater nuance and subtlety in the meaning of the lyrics. Crosby learned to 'play the microphone' like an instrument, and soon everyone did.

In just the same way as new technologies extend the possibilities of vaulting and singing, so they can influence thinking and imagining. The invention of writing and drawing enabled people to hold their thoughts steady, in an externalized draft, and reflect upon them, and that changed the way they thought – and we think. It also allowed a different type of collective thinking: scholarship would hardly exist as an activity if we were not able to ponder on other people's frozen thoughts, and reply to them with our own. Fictional and biographical literature allows us to imaginatively enter other worlds, and to explore – in a new off-line, reflective sort of way – our own emotional reactions to the predicaments they portray.

Samuel Richardson's *Clarissa*, published in the 1740s, was probably the first novel to depict the everyday interiority of consciousness, and contemporary novelist and academic David Lodge has argued that the book both evoked and demanded a new kind of sensibility on the part of the reader.[7] It was the start of a new development in what Howard Gardner called inter- and intrapersonal intelligence that now makes it seem perfectly 'natural' and easy to read a contemporary novel full of introspection, such as Ian McEwan's *Saturday*; but it would have felt very unnatural in the early eighteenth century.

Technology and intelligence

Today, some of the most important mind-expanding technologies involve visual and digital media. As we surf the internet, play with a Wii, watch MTV or an interactive DVD or a show like the *X Factor*, we are learning the conventions of each format, and that learning may, in turn, alter how we interpret and approach the world more generally. To cope with abrupt cutting from close-ups to long shots, switching between storylines (as in *The Sopranos*, for instance), watching split-screen action and filling in missing information (where you can't ask for clarification) requires new mental skills and attitudes.

Gavriel Salomon has shown that young people differ in how well they have mastered these skills, and also that interaction with different forms of media develops the relevant skills to higher levels. And these skills and sensibilities can come to influence perception and thinking more broadly. A student in one of Salomon's studies commented: 'I have learned to think of my life as a series of frames partly overlapping each other and dissolving into each other.'[8]

Each new technology creates winners and losers. In the Middle Ages, troubadours used to rove around the countryside 'singing the news'; but the invention of the printing press eventually put most of them out of work. 'Talking pictures' were bad news for cinema organists. But it is not only social groups and occupations that go up and down with technology. Each innovation may invite the development of new instruments of intelligence; and at the same time it may neglect or sideline others. What Salomon calls one's 'cognitive-representational arsenal' may not only be enriched but also potentially skewed. Music videos and *Sesame Street* can cultivate both a facility with and an appetite for fast-paced, glitzy, bitty kinds of presentation. Salomon has written about what he calls the 'butterfly defect', a shallow flightiness of attention induced by too much internet-surfing and MTV-watching.

These shifts in the attentional habits of young people have caused widespread alarm. Two recent books by American academics are apocalyptically entitled *Distracted: The Erosion of Attention and the Coming Dark Age*, and *The Dumbest Generation: How the Digital Age Stupefies Young Americans and Jeopardizes Our Future*.[9] But digital technologies do not *necessarily* undermine the ability and pleasure in slower, more detailed and painstaking kinds of learning – there is no reason why the strengthening of one kind of attention should automatically weaken others – but they may do. It depends partly on the early diet of attention-shaping activities that a child gets used to, and partly on the frame of mind in which they engage with different technologies.

It is useful here to clarify the distinction between the effects *with* and *of* technology.[10] Working with a calculator, or a 3D graphical software package, a skilled user is capable of doing things they could not do without, and doing them with far greater speed and far less mental effort. But once they have got used to such tools, what happens when you take them away? What are the cognitive residues that are left behind? Has your experience with the calculator made you better at mental arithmetic, or worse? Is your resilience in the face of difficulty stronger or weaker? Has your ability to make sensible 'guesstimates' of the kind of answer you are looking for got better or worse? These are the effects *of* technology, and it is with these that education has, presumably, to be concerned. As teachers, we cannot know what tools will be available to our students throughout their lifetimes. So we have to think about the effects that our activities are having on the core habits of mind that constitute their on-board software. Whatever technological advances are made, there will always be a need for this intelligent core. As Salomon et al. say:

> Dilemmas and questions such as 'How much more should I prepare for the test?' and 'What will my readers think of this argument?' ... need an independent and capable thinking mind, not one that constantly depends on technology, intelligent as it may be.[11]

One disposition that will significantly moderate the power of distributed intelligence is what we might call *resourcefulness*; that is, an abiding tendency to be on the look-out for tools and resources with which to amplify one's intelligence. You may be surrounded by all kinds of smart tools, but if you are not disposed to make use of them, they might as well not be there.

Writers on distributed intelligence often talk of the affordances of different tools. A chair affords sitting; a pad of paper affords writing; a friend affords conversation; and so on. But the idea of an affordance is as much subjective as objective. Different species 'see' different affordance in the same room. An upright chair affords *sitting* to us, but also *sleeping* and *washing* to a cat, and maybe (if there are a few stray crumbs) *eating* to a fly. There is a delightful article, published by Jakob von Uexkull in the 1930s, called 'A stroll through the worlds of animals and men', in which he illustrates what the world of affordances might look like to different species. You would be amazed how different things look to a scallop![12]

The perception of some of these affordances is built-in. But whether a credit card affords *cutting* – when you realize, in the middle of your picnic, that you have forgotten to bring a knife for the cheese – is a more personal matter of perceptiveness and ingenuity. One picnicker may have a more flexible and creative sense of resourcefulness than the others. Being able to escape from what Karl Duncker,[13] in his series of experiments in the 1940s, famously referred to as 'functional fixedness' – the inability to see more than the most obvious or habitual affordances – has to become a key educational aim for a teacher who takes the idea of distributed intelligence seriously. As Luis Moll has put it, 'A goal of the teacher is to teach the children how to exploit the resources in their environment, how to become conscious users of the cultural resources available for thinking, be it a book, their bilingualism, the library, or other children.'[14]

Extending the mind

What is emerging from all these studies is, again, a very different view of intelligence from the hyper-rational, all-in-your-head model with which we began our journey. Being intelligent depends on the tools you have to hand, how well you have accommodated your own mind and body to their potential, and the broader impact that such accommodation may have had on the way you relate to the world. Intelligence is no longer a personal possession, locked up in the recesses of private reasoning; it loops out into the world in dozens of useful ways.

That is what psychologists mean when they talk about 'the extended mind'. That is why we have to talk about intelligence as distributed, not as localized within individual skulls. And that is why, as Luis Moll says, it is the job of the educator not to make children dependent on digital tools, nor to deprive them of them, but to help them develop their tool-mindedness, and the ability to use tools to expand their own internal capacity, as well as to get interesting things done.

> **"Intelligence is no longer a personal possession, locked up in the recesses of private reasoning; it loops out into the world in dozens of useful ways."**

But new tools are not all, or always, good news. As we discover their affordances, and adapt to be able to make use of them, so unforeseen problems and dilemmas may emerge. Digital tools such as the internet make available amounts of information that would have been unimaginable even ten years ago. But is it *good* information? How do you know that Wikipedia is telling you the truth? If resourcefulness is one key disposition, when it comes to making the best use of tools and technology, intelligent *scepticism* is another. Perhaps education in the twenty-first century ought to be doing more to cultivate such scepticism.

But there is a deeper issue than scepticism. As well as being able to tell whether information is reliable, it is becoming increasingly important to develop a good sense of whether it is *wholesome*. There is a mass of images and information available at the click of a mouse that is not just of dubious validity, but morally repugnant as well. Before the internet, it was easier to protect children from pornography, for example. The traditional 'top shelf' of the local newsagent contains mild stuff indeed compared with what thousands of 9-year-olds have already watched on the net.

We talked briefly in the last chapter about the basic emotional systems, one of which was the Disgust System, designed to keep out or expel noxious material and experiences. Though each of these systems is inherently valuable, what triggers them, and the ways they are expressed, are heavily modified by cultural learning. Young people learn from their families, and then from their peers, what to be fearful of, angry about, or disgusted by. There is a real risk that peer pressure to be 'cool' and 'unfazed' leads to a dampening of the Disgust System, and the inability to be properly, appropriately revolted or outraged by disgusting things. The issue is not where moral lines should be drawn so much as what the social and personal effects are of losing the use of the Disgust System in the Digital Age. This is a clear example of how new tools may raise all kinds of complex and unforeseen issues. Schools as well as families need to find ways of grasping such moral nettles.

Starting out

Education has always made use of tools to help students think and learn. It is very hard to do long division in your head: if you don't happen to have a calculator, at least you need a piece of paper and a pen – and some distant memories of how you set out long division on the page. As you divide 4385 by 17, your brain, your hand, your pen and your notebook all work seamlessly together, the page being able to hold information that you could not hold in mind at the same time as you are performing the mental arithmetic that you know how to do.

Then came useful visual tools like Venn diagrams and 'mind maps'. The former helped work out tricky logic like 'All marines are brave; some marines are not married; so some married people are not brave'. The latter helped to organize and structure what you knew about France or neuropeptides. Some teachers used these tools to help students become more aware and sophisticated in their learning. They made them think about when it helped to use a mind map, and for what purposes. They invited students to experiment with different ways of designing them for different jobs, and to talk about their explorations and discoveries with others in the class. But others tended to 'teach mind maps' as if they were good for everything and there was only one Right Way to do it.

Guy asked a relation of his, Charlotte, when she was about 11, if she had 'done mind maps' in her school. She said yes, and offered to draw him one. It was a beautiful map of the animal kingdom: all the lines were the right length, and words like 'invertebrates' spelled correctly. Guy was impressed – and a little suspicious. 'Have you done that one before?' he asked her. 'Oh yes, lots', said Charlotte. 'That's our teacher's favourite!'. When he suggested they did a new one that she hadn't done before, there was a long pause, and Charlotte said awkwardly, 'I think I'll go out and play on the trampo-line now . . .' She clearly hadn't learned to think about the pros and cons of mind maps, nor to see herself as the intelligent constructor and user of mind maps to help her think, learn and remember useful things. She has just learned to do a few. And that to us seems like a waste of a useful little tool (and of a bright girl's time).

The same kind of consideration applies to the use of computers in schools. An intermediate school one of us visited in New Zealand had two smart new computer suites next door to each other. In one room, small groups of 12-year-olds were exploring the potential of an advanced desk top publishing package – way ahead of what most adults could do – and discussing how they could use it to present projects they were working on in science. In the identical room next door, individual 12-year-olds were sitting at screens, working their way through graded mathematical exercises of the most traditional kind. In the first room, youngsters were using the tool to stretch their powers of imagination, collaboration and communication; and they were being thoughtful about what the tool was good for and what not. In the second, students were doing exactly the same kind of 'sequestered problem solving' that were the stock-in-trade of teachers in days gone by.

Going deeper

In the computer lab at St Boniface's Secondary Boys' School in Plymouth, mixed groups of Year 8s, 9s and 10s (12- to 15-year-olds) are working together on a project called ASPIRE. Their task is to design a website that will encourage other secondary students to think about the future of education, and about how to design schools that would prepare them better for life as they imagine it will be.

First, they have to design the site, and then to populate it with a wide range of games, quizzes and 'provocations' that would help to stimulate imaginative thinking and talking. There are varying degrees of sophistication in the way different groups are tackling this challenge. Some of the younger students are finding it hard to think beyond wanting comfier chairs and better vending machines. Others have just been gently shown that they are assuming that all they have to do was think how *they* wanted school to be, post their ideas on the website, and hope the rest of the world would agree with them.

But others have already gone deeper. One group is realizing that their first attempts are rather 'boy-ish', and that not all the visitors to their site – girls, sixth formers (students in their last two years at school), or those from different cultures, for example – might be engaged by the same kinds of games that appeal to them. Their self-discovered task now is to think about how to engage different kinds of audiences in different kinds of ways, and they are struggling with great intelligence and commitment to escape the gravitational field of their own interests and backgrounds. As new thoughts and questions arise, so they are able to go back to the internet and search for other sites, and begin to explore whether there might be partners in different kinds of schools, in different parts of the world, that would help them improve their site. By bringing digital tools into school in creative ways that engage with young people's desires to do 'real things', the tools are enabling them to stretch and strengthen their own powers of intelligence.

A final example draws on Ellen Langer's research at Harvard into what she calls 'could be language'. In a number of studies, Langer has found that, if you present information in a tentative, provisional kind of way, students are much better able to use that information thoughtfully and creatively. Show a class a funny-shaped bit of rubber and say 'This *could be* a dog's chewy toy', and they are subsequently much more likely to see that it could also be used as a pencil eraser when the need arises. In other words, 'could be language' invites a more imaginative, productive and sceptical attitude towards what one is being told – exactly the attitudes that we said earlier are so important for young people to develop as they meet all sorts of knowledge claims on the internet.[15]

Once teachers see this, it is usually easy for them to adopt a more 'could be' tone towards their own teaching. But it may need a nudge, like encountering Ellen Langer's work, for that shift to occur. One of us was chatting with a group of secondary school History teachers not long ago, and they got on to complaining about how credulous and uncritical their students were when they got onto the internet. 'They just take everything on Wikipedia at face value', one said in exasperation. We enquired politely whether they were absolutely sure that the way they were doing the Tudors, or the Causes of the First World War, was inviting and strengthening exactly the kind of intelligent scepticism towards knowledge claims that they were now bewailing the lack of. They admitted that there might be scope for them to be rather more 'could be' in their teaching style. It is our view that schools are more likely to be effective at expanding young people's real-world intelligence if they adjust these kinds of background assumptions and habits, than if they try to import glossy new 'thinking skills' programmes.

A useful tool: the Person-Plus Tool Kit

Intelligent learners need practice in being resourceful – being on the look-out for tools and resources with which to make them more powerful learners.

Get the class to brainstorm all the things they use to help them extend their skills and master tricky ideas. Establish a regular classroom routine: The Tool Check. 'OK everyone; just stop and explore with your neighbour for a minute what things and resources could help you with your learning right now.'

Get the students to create, and keep adding to, a visual display or poster of all the resources they could draw on to help them learn, headed:

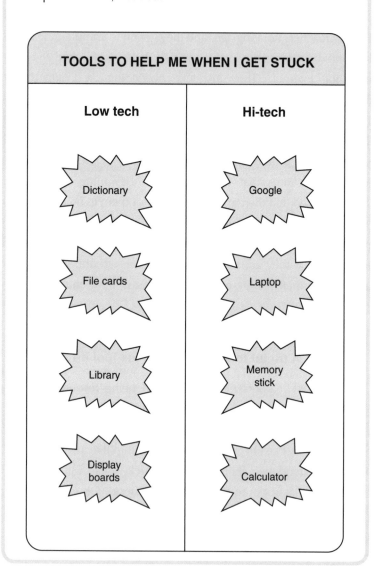

TOOLS TO HELP ME WHEN I GET STUCK

Low tech

Dictionary

File cards

Library

Display boards

Hi-tech

Google

Laptop

Memory stick

Calculator

Ideas into practice

Many schools remain strangely suspicious of tools, especially if they were not around at the time teachers were growing up! If David Beckham were to present himself we could easily find ourselves asking him to remove his football boots and sit down to a pen and paper test to take an assessment of his skill before realizing just how ridiculous this would be!

To help you think how you might try out ideas about distributed intelligence, you might like to wonder:

1 How could I explore with students their 'tool dependencies'? What could they do without? How would they manage without certain tools?

2 To what extent has technology been a force for good or ill? Perhaps I could ask colleagues and young people alike for their views.

3 How could I help students and teachers to see tools differently, perhaps by introducing specific tools – both high- and low-tech – and asking students to undertake similar tasks using them?

4 How would the exam system need to change if we took our responsibility to develop 'tool consciousness' more seriously? Are there ways in which even in tests that I administer I am being unnecessarily restrictive in the way I allow students to use tools?

5 Could I get students (and my colleagues) thinking and talking more about the development of tools in history,

science, maths and PE, for example, listing those which they feel are integral to intelligent activity in the subject?

6 How can we cultivate 'intelligent scepticism' in young learners without taking away their enthusiasm?

7 How could I create a classroom experience of under-taking various tasks with and without familiar tools and reflect on the different experiences?

6

Intelligence is Social

> Intelligence is a social triumph, which reveals our debt to
> earlier generations, other cultures, teachers, professors,
> parents and the TV set. Collective intelligence involves a
> major change in the way we think about the relationship
> between the individual and society, and consequently
> the way we organise our schools.
>
> Phil Brown and Hugh Lauder[1]

Have you ever wondered just how valuable social interaction can be? Researcher Oscar Ybarra and colleagues at the University of Michigan[2] decided they would find out by conducting two experiments. First, they surveyed 3610 people between the ages of 24 and 96 to establish their patterns of social interaction. They gave each person a widely used test of mental function and, after controlling for variables, they looked at the connection between frequency of social contact and mental function. It turned out that the more social contact subjects had, the better their cognitive functioning was.

Emboldened by this finding, the researchers then compared the respective benefits of various kinds of activities on college students. Each student was allocated to one of three groups. The first group had a discussion about a social issue for ten minutes. The second undertook tasks such as a comprehension test and a crossword puzzle. And the third, the control group, watched a ten-minute extract from *Seinfeld*. All the students then undertook tests of their mental processing and working memory. The results showed that students who spent ten minutes talking about an issue boosted their cognitive performance just as much as those who took part in more obviously intellectual activities. This research suggests that, such is the power of social interaction, just ten minutes spent talking with others can enhance mental performance.

> "When it comes to being intelligent it is clear that there is much more than simply what we can do as an individual; how we interact with others is a crucial element of how smart we are in the real world."

When it comes to being intelligent it is clear that there is much more than simply what we can do as an individual; how we interact with others is a crucial element of how smart we are in the real world. Intelligence *is* social, for the most part arising in groups. Yet for years we measured intelligence on an individual basis and it is individual students rather than groups who take tests and examinations in schools. Indeed, collaborative work in school is still tainted with the idea that it might, somehow be a kind of cheating. And school reports focus on individual students, too, only tending to note social skills when they appear to be in short supply. Rampant individualism has for too long undervalued more social and communitarian perspectives. The same culture of individualism pervades society beyond school, especially in countries like the USA, Australia, the UK and Canada.

Where once we talked of *human capital*, thinking that the goal of education was to create lots of clever individuals, we now need to think in terms of *social capital*, recognizing that talent does not exist in isolation. Today's children are growing up in a socially networked world. YouTube, FaceBook and MSN Messenger are just three current examples of the online social spaces in which young people spend much of their time. Using the internet it is even possible to play collaborative games talking to other players across the world as you do so, as well as the more traditionally competitive ones. The world has never been a more networked place, yet for the most part schools remain stubbornly focused on individuals. In the UK, this individualism has recently gained particular force through the determined use of the phrase 'personalized learning'.[3] Of course it's helpful to focus more precisely on the needs of individual learners, but maybe we need a parallel initiative for 'socialized learning' too.

> **"**Of course it's helpful to focus more precisely on the needs of individual learners, but maybe we need a parallel initiative for 'socialized learning' too.**"**

Creativity expert Charles Leadbeater[4] has recently explored the impact of the Web on the way we view the world and concludes that the current generation's minds are being shaped by life in virtual worlds and on social networking sites. He concludes that young minds are as much social as individual: 'They will look for information themselves and expect and welcome opportunities to participate, collaborate, share and work with their peers.' It seems impossible that schools can continue to resist this growing pattern of social interaction in the ways they structure learning and assessment. They will surely have to change their attitude to knowledge, valuing the capacity to collaborate at least as highly as the ability to sit in isolation on a hot summer day and heroically regurgitate data in a timed essay.

So in this chapter we explore the ways in which intelligence and much learning are essentially social concepts. We will look at the ways in which intelligence is distributed among people and how smart people and smart groups are able to access the brainpower of those around them. We will remind ourselves of the necessity of behaving reciprocally and of the ways in which intelligence is, in a powerful sense, socially contagious. Any really intelligent action, we will suggest, requires us to be aware of the effect of our actions on others.

Getting to grips with social intelligence

First, let's unpack a little of the history of social intelligence. Arguably the father of social intelligence is Edward Thorndike.[5] As early as 1920, Edward Thorndike talked of social intelligence as being able to 'act wisely in human relations'. The best known proponent of the social view of the mind, however, is Lev Vygotsky.[6] Vygotsky wrote in the first part of the twentieth century, although much of his work was not available in English until later. He helped us to see just how much of learning is socially constructed. In a direct challenge to Piaget (who saw young learners as only being able to act in certain ways once they had reached specific developmental stages), Vygotsky suggests that social learning actually *precedes* development. 'Every function in the child's cultural development appears twice: first on the social level, and later, on the individual level; first between people (interpsychological) and then inside the child (intrapsychological).' Knowledge, Vygotsky argues, is something that we construct socially through our interactions with our peers and with those who are more knowledgeable than ourselves.

The role of imitation

Indeed, much learning takes place by a process of imitation. A student watches the way one of her peers answers a difficult question and tries to do it similarly. And teachers offer templates – techniques, tools, patterns of behaviour – for students to copy and make their own. In America, the role of imitation in the development of intelligent behaviour was championed by Albert Bandura. He explored the way we observe behaviour and its outcomes and then imitate (or avoid) what we observe. In Bandura's analysis we cannot escape the fact that we are all learning role models for each other. (And, therefore, in the classroom hierarchy what the teacher does or does not do is a powerful force.)

Bandura described the conditions necessary for effective imitation and modelling. First of all, the learner must notice what is being modelled. Then she must remember and retain what has been noticed. And finally she must be able *and* willing to reproduce a desired behaviour. As Bandura nicely put it:

Learning would be exceedingly laborious, not to mention hazardous, if people had to rely solely on the effects of their own actions to inform them what to do. Fortunately, most human behaviour is learned observationally through modelling: from observing others one forms an idea of how new behaviours are performed, and on later occasions this coded information serves as a guide for action.[7]

Interestingly, neuroscience has recently begun to give tantalising insights into what may be going on in the brain while we are watching others. Special kinds of brain cells called 'mirror neurons' exist which are not only activated when we are performing an action but also fire up when we watch others doing something similar. Our brains, it would seem, are wired to notice and imitate others. More than this, research[8] is suggesting that not only do our brains notice what others are doing, and activate the neural circuits we might use if we were performing the same action, they are also able to read the intentions (the 'why') behind what they see. Even young children do not just imitate what they observe; they discern the purpose behind the observed action, and take that into account in determining when and how to copy it.

In psychology, there is also a field of research known as 'social contagion' which seeks to explain the way in which behaviour can be 'caught' (like a contagious disease) merely by being exposed to other people. There is an emerging consensus that two kinds of responses can be caught in this way. The first can be summed up by the word 'mood' and the second by 'behaviour'.

As any teacher knows, some lessons go better because somehow the mood of the group is right. Or the overall mood can shift as a consequence of a change in just a few individuals being 'caught' by others in the class. In terms of behaviour, social contagion theory can be used to explain copycat activities in any group. An outbreak of teenage suicides in a town called Bridgend in Wales is a sad example of this phenomenon. Equally it can be used to help to account for collective displays of altruism such as when ordinary people take to the streets in aid of a cause in which they have not previously shown interest.

Is intelligence itself contagious? Certainly the evidence would suggest that peer groups and attendant social pressure are significant variables in our chances of success in life. But can you catch intelligence from others? We surmise that in some senses of the word you can. Simply by being with people who are expert at 'reading' social situations (or able to make best use of the kinds of tools we were exploring in the last chapter, for example), you are more likely to be able to function intelligently yourself. The great American educator John Dewey, for example, argued strongly for a more cooperative approach to learning, variously using phrases like 'cooperative intelligence' and 'collective intelligence'. Dewey explained this by suggesting that: 'The self only achieves mind in the degree to which knowledge of things is incarnate in the life about him; the self is not a separate mind building up knowledge on its own account.'[9] In other words, for knowledge to be in any real sense useful, it has to have expression in relationships and social activity. No man (or woman) is an island.

Bringing this way of thinking up to date, British educationists Phil Brown and Hugh Lauder (whose words began this chapter) argue compellingly that the concept of collective intelligence is a powerful metaphor and potential solution for explaining the continuing social inequalities which exist in education. Configure an education system around the notion of collective intelligence and you make a powerful statement about your desire to help young people learn how to organize themselves to solve shared problems as well as developing themselves.

> **"For knowledge to be in any real sense useful, it has to have expression in relationships and social activity. No man (or woman) is an island."**

Communities of practice

Through the research undertaken by Jean Lave and Etienne Wenger,[10] we now have a much better understanding of not just the social elements of learning but also the way in which learning is situated in a particular context. How we learn on a sports field, in a science lab or in a drama studio is heavily influenced by the social situation and by the nature of the activity in which we are engaged. The way learning is organized in a school maths class, a competitive sports team, a rock band or an amateur dramatic society is very different, and these cultural differences strongly influence how people grow and think.

Contexts really matter. Lave and Wenger coined a useful phrase, 'communities of practice', to describe the kinds of social learning that such cultures require. Members of a community pursue a common interest and help each other as they do so. And as they work and solve problems together, so their learning habits and attitudes rub off on each other. New members watch carefully how the more established members talk, respond and deal with challenges, like children do when they want to join someone's 'gang'. Lave and Wenger have called this stage of joining a community 'legitimate peripheral participation'.

The noun 'practice' (in the phrase 'communities of practice') reminds us of the verb 'practise'. As we become part of a group or community we necessarily go through a kind of apprenticeship in which we gradually learn how to do something. To do this we practise with others, learning from those more skilled (closer to the 'centre' of the community) than ourselves in their repertoires and insights. Practice also suggests that learning is a process not an event; it takes time. The medical student slowly develops her clinical skill, and also gradually grows into the roles and identities she sees in her more senior or experienced colleagues – a process the French refer to as the *déformation professionelle*.

Learning here is much more in the relationship between people than in any one individual's head. Learning is to be found in the conversations and interactions of a community rather than somehow belonging to an individual. Young people (and adults) are necessarily part of many communities of practice. If you are a teacher reading *New Kinds of Smart*, then this is one obvious community to which you belong (especially if you are preparing for a seminar on it!). But there will be many other 'clubs' you belong to, each with its own ways of thinking and acting, such as families, 'mother and baby groups', sports clubs, music groups, soap-opera watchers, walking groups, faith-based communities and internet chat rooms.

There are many implications for schools here. Assuming that you want students to become part of the community of practice called 'school', then, as Barbara Rogoff and Jean Lave[11] have observed, you are likely to want to invest effort in ensuring that you offer 'instruction that builds on children's interests in a collaborative way'. From her work on informal learning, largely in non-Western settings, Rogoff has developed a useful phrase, 'observing and pitching in', to describe the way in which learners (younger family members, for example) watch their elders attentively and then, when they are ready, 'pitch in' or try things out for themselves.

This is just one kind of legitimate peripheral participation and you will be able to think of the many ways in which those you teach move from the periphery of the learning communities they belong to – both in school and out – towards the centre. Rogoff emphasizes the contrast between 'intent community participation' (the observing and pitching in mentioned above) and 'assembly-line instruction' (the kind of factory-based approaches to teaching and learning prevalent in too many classroom cultures).

Chris Watkins[12] has taken the idea of a community of practice and explicitly applied it to the classroom. In a deliberate attempt to move away from the paradigm that says 'learning = being taught' he has homed in on the fact that the way a classroom is managed is a more significant variable than any other in terms of helping learning.[13] Taking this as his starting point, he has sought to identify those elements of practice in the classroom community which are most beneficial for learning. Watkins describes three stages in the development of learning communities:

1 Classrooms as *communities*, where the teacher is building a sense of community in which students are actively engaged and have a chance to shape the way things are organized.

2 Classrooms as *communities of learners*, where the spotlight is on learning (rather than on, say, teaching). There is likely to be an emphasis on students generating their own questions, high levels of interaction between students and good levels of engagement.

3 Classrooms as *learning communities*, in which the emphasis is on the active creation of knowledge by all concerned, including the teacher. Watkins explains, 'A classroom run as a learning community operates on the understanding that the growth of knowledge involves individual and social processes.' In such contexts, learners not only take responsibility for themselves and their peers but also for what *needs* to be known. By the same token,

learners are encouraged to see knowledge not as something that is static nor even solely something that is 'what the teacher has lots of' but as something that they themselves can help to create.

Anyone in any doubt about the influence of learning communities on student outcomes needs only to think of the implicit power of role modelling which has been a thread in this chapter so far. We know, for example, that, as well as the teacher and other adults in any classroom, the peer or social groups to which learners choose to attach themselves in school have a huge impact on their learning lives.

> "As well as the teacher and other adults in any classroom, the peer or social groups to which learners choose to attach themselves in school have a huge impact on their learning lives."

Thomas Kinderman[14] has shown the degree to which the peer groups children naturally choose in school can enhance or undermine their motivation in school. He also discovered a kind of social contagion taking place with regard to motivation, with newer members adopting the level of motivation of others in their group by association. These kinds of findings are exciting but also challenging precisely because we are talking about children's naturally chosen social groups rather than any to which teachers or parents have 'assigned' them.

Taking the idea of social intelligence to a wider audience

Stepping out of the school into the complex interactions of everyday life, Daniel Goleman has recently popularized the concept of social intelligence in similar vein to his earlier writing about emotional intelligence.[15] Goleman organizes his definition of social intelligence into two categories, social awareness and social facility:

1 Social awareness:

   (a) Primal empathy – picking up non-verbal signals.

   (b) Attunement – listening fully and receptively.

   (c) Empathic accuracy – understanding the thoughts, feelings and intentions of others.

   (d) Social cognition – knowing how social groups work.

2 Social facility:

   (a) Synchrony – smooth interacting at the non-verbal level.

   (b) Self-presentation – effective self-presentation.

   (c) Influence – shaping outcomes during a social interaction.

   (d) Concern – caring about the needs of others and acting accordingly.

These eight elements provide a useful focus for the kind of dispositions one might be trying to cultivate in the classroom as well as those attributes that will characterize socially intelligent adults throughout their lives. Growing up is, as Nicholas Humphrey has suggested, a kind of 'social chess'.[16] Children are constantly, as the metaphor suggests, learning to look beneath the surface of those around them to figure out the intentions of their families, teachers, friends and enemies. We neglect this aspect of intelligence at our peril and the challenge to schools now must be how to develop it more effectively. We saw in the last chapter just how important tools are to a fully intelligent person; the same is true for those most important of all 'tools', the people around us. This was true when we lived in tribes on the savannah. It is even more true in the age of the online social network[17] (although the fact that you are in a particular social network may or may not make you collectively more intelligent in and of itself!).

One of the best-known and most detailed descriptions of social intelligence in action has been provided by cognitive anthropologist Edwin Hutchins.[18] Hutchins explored the way in which a naval ship is navigated in and out of a harbour and noted the extraordinary way in which intelligence is distributed among the different people on board. Two people take visual sightings. They call their readings out to two other sailors who, in turn, relay them by telephone to the bridge. Other people use specialized instruments and maps to plot the ship's progress and check on relative position to known landmarks. Thus a course is steered with a new set of data being relayed every few moments. No one individual could manage alone, because nobody is in possession of all the information needed – there is no individual 'in charge'. A sophisticated piece of problem-solving relies on each member of the team doing their bit at the right time, and passing their vital scrap of information on to the right person. The ship sails smoothly into harbour through the distributed social intelligence of its crew. As in Chris Watkins' learning community, it is not just that people are being intelligent and socially aware *in* a group; the intelligence emerges from the coordinated efforts of the group itself.

Starting out

Since the 1960s UK schools have moved away from classes sitting in rows facing their teacher and only speaking once spoken to. Go into many schools and wander past classrooms and you will see children learning not just through the endeavour of their teacher (in lecturing mode) but also by working in a small group with others. In early years this is very common. In primary education it is widespread. In secondary education the use of group work and discussion are more patchily distributed, with some subject disciplines being more likely to favour such interaction than others. In one study, English and science teachers were found to use small groups more frequently than mathematics teachers, for example.[19] But all teachers surveyed identified a variety of learning purposes for small group work. These included:

- stimulating, pooling and developing ideas;
- planning, carrying out, analysing and evaluating practical work;
- verbalizing thinking to clarify and improve understanding; and
- engaging students actively in their learning.

But a visitor to schools in different parts of the world will see huge variation in the way that group work is used. It can be focused, dynamic, creative and the spawning ground for socially intelligent pupils. Equally it can be lazy, unfocused and introduced in such a way that it is clearly seen by the powers that be as less valuable than individual work where you can be more confident as to 'who is contributing the real ideas'. In the second kind of example there still may lurk the assumption that somehow working in groups is a form of cheating, where less able children steal the ideas of their smarter peers.

Something called SEAL (Social and Emotional Aspects of Learning) is now widely used in English schools. Its core materials are very much about developing the kind of social intelligence as defined by Goleman, and there are many useful materials in this programme of curriculum development. Too often, however, SEAL is seen as a way to 'lessen the undesirable', rather than as a vital form of education for all. And as almost all learning has social and emotional components, learning these in isolation in separate courses as part of SEAL can make such aspects of learning, paradoxically, seem marginal. Unless there is a culture across the school which values the social aspects of learning, both in formal and informal settings, the powerful pull of individualism is likely to triumph.

Going deeper

Two interesting approaches to the cultivation of social intelligence are beginning to take root in schools, both emanating from the USA. The first is a programme known as Fostering Communities of Learners and has been elegantly described by researcher Ann Brown.[20] As she puts it: 'Mind is inside the head, but it is also with others.'

Using an approach to learning known as 'jigsaw groups'[21] (see below), Brown gets students to tackle big complex topics (such as the ecology of animals and their habitats) and requires a class to work as a network of communities of inquiry. The approach creates a learning environment in which students are compelled to collaborate. Small groups carry out their own research (each being given different topics such as predator–prey relations or food gathering, for example). But every so often the class reconfigures into jigsaw groups containing representatives from each of the research groups, who share their progress and their questions, and carry ideas back to their research groups about how to make further progress. Pupils in Brown's classrooms did better on standard tests than others in more conventional situations, recording significant and sustained improvements and demonstrating prowess normally associated with much older students.

A useful tool: the jigsaw technique

1   Select a juicy topic with information, opinion and other material which can be split into five or six different batches.

2   Divide a class into five or six different groups.

3   Give each group different information.

4   Set the class tasks which require each group first to understand the material they have, then to share it with others.

5   Encourage groups to take the initiative and approach another group with questions to help them with their learning.

6   From time to time stop and hear interim presentations from individual groups.

7   Bring the whole project to a close with some kind of whole class display, writing or presentation.

Another idea increasingly being used both in teacher development which could also be modified for use in classrooms is Open Space (OS). Created by Harrison Owen,[22] OS is a method of running largely self-organized meetings or sessions to ensure maximum engagement and discussion about issues that matter to those present. Although initially used in the early 1990s by adults, largely as a reaction against conferences which overwhelm participants with too many presentations from the stage and too many 'workshops' which are really lectures, OS could equally be used in schools.

The term 'open space' implies that the most productive conversations and the most stimulating learning take place in the gaps *between* what has been planned by way of input. People, in other words, create knowledge when they interact together, and because they need to exercise their social intelligence to contribute to any session, so that they in turn reap most benefit. The process typically looks like this:

> 1   The class sits in a circle, a good engaging topic is introduced and initial discussion takes place to check that everyone is happy and understands.

⇩

> 2   Individuals offer to lead a discussion or activity session.

⇩

> 3   A rough timetable is drawn up using different spaces in the room.

	Window	By white board	Corridor
11.30–12.00			
12.00–12.30			
12.30–13.00			

⇩

> 4 Ideas are then reduced to the number of time slots available and written on to the timetable.

⇩

> 5 Sessions then take place. Hosts must remain in place; others may choose to stay or move around.

Open Space is a free-form engagement. It has few rules. The 'rules', such as they are, are expressed, in somewhat folksy language, as four principles and a 'law'.

Four Principles

1 Whoever comes are the right people.

2 Whatever happens is the only thing that could have.

3 Whenever it starts is the right time.

4 When it's over, it's over.

The Law of Two Feet

If, during the course of the gathering, any person finds him or herself in a situation where they are neither learning nor contributing, they must use their two feet and go to some more productive place.

Open Space puts the onus on individuals to invest in creating their own agendas and seeing through their own trains of thought. When it works, it is exhilarating. But it is not for the faint-hearted and needs careful planning. For those already using approaches like Philosophy for Children where groups of students are encouraged to question each other in a fairly fluid environment, OS will seem an obvious extension to this.

Of course, the idea of sitting round a table together even in a classroom is not a new one. In the 1930s, philanthropist Edward Harkness gave money to various New England schools to create a different kind of classroom, one in which the focus was on collaboration and cooperation, where teachers and students gather around an oval table together to share information, explore ideas, develop questions, and learn together. This kind of table is now known as a Harkness table.

The tables don't have a head or a foot, top or bottom. They were designed so everyone can participate and contribute as equals with the teacher participating on the same level. Students tackle questions from every angle, and, through discussion, discover that there aren't always concrete right or wrong answers. Their own understanding becomes deeper and more subtle, so that, through using the intelligence of the group, each member's own intelligence is enhanced.

Traditional model   Harkness model

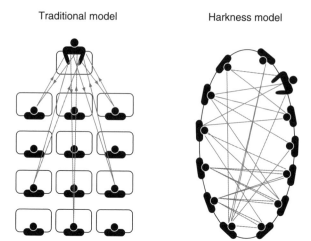

Figure 6.1 The Harkness model of teaching

If social intelligence is to be of real-world use, then it has to be developed out of school as well as in. As Jean Lave puts it:

> There is a reason to suspect that what we call cognition is in fact a complex social phenomenon . . . Cognition observed in everyday practice is distributed – stretched over, not divided among – mind, body, activity and culturally organised settings which include other actors.[23]

If teachers and school leaders believe this – and we think there is good reason for them to – then finding more opportunities for social learning in and out of school to merge and for enquiries to move between home, community and school becomes highly desirable.

Ideas into practice

Intelligence is social. It very often arises collectively, as people work, learn and play together. Yet still schools tend to undervalue it. Maybe they just find it too difficult to organize, control and measure. Young people who are talking, arguing and exploring together are likely to generate their own enthusiasm and engagement – but they are also likely to go 'off-piste' as far as the exam syllabus is concerned – and that may too risky or inconvenient to allow.

To help you think how you might try out ideas about social intelligence, you might like to wonder:

1 Would it would be helpful to replicate the Oscar Ybarra experiment and build regular moments into the school day when our students are given ten minutes to talk about an issue?

2 Could I set up a version of the research on 'cognition in the wild' created by Edwin Hutchins, perhaps focusing on running a school as the model (rather than steering a ship)?

3 How could we best help learners see the value of cooperative working? Could we introducing specific rewards or encouragement for effective reciprocal teaching and learning? How would we square doing that, when many educational systems still reward individual attainment?

4 How best might I create a classroom which really is a

community of learning and in which learners really experience a sense of creating new knowledge? What small steps could I take next week to move in that direction?

5 Would it be possible to try using a Harkness table, or at least using teaching approaches where I am sitting around a large table with learners rather than standing at the front?

6 Could I engage colleagues in learning how to use either the Jigsaw or Open Space approaches? Which kinds of lesson topics might work best for trying out these approaches?

7 How can we help students carry their social intelligence more fluidly back and forth between school and their out-of-school lives?

7

Intelligence is Strategic

Here is Edward Bear, coming downstairs, now, bump,
bump, bump, on the back of his head behind Christopher
Robin. It is as far as he knows the only way of coming
downstairs, but somewhere he feels there is another way,
if only he could stop for a moment and think of it.

A.A. Milne[1]

Try this. Using these items – a candle, a box of tacks and a book of matches – can you attach the candle to a wall so that it will not drip on the table below? If you are like most people you will try to nail the candle to the wall or possibly melt some of the candle's wax and use this to glue it shakily to the wall. In a classic experiment, Karl Duncker found that very few participants thought of using the *box* the tacks were in as the candleholder. The explanation for this is that they had not thought of the box as being a candleholder because they were so used to seeing it as a container (see page 132 for the problem and 133 for the solution).

Known as 'functional fixedness', the candle/box problem

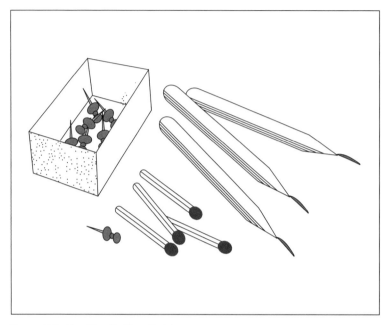

Figure 7.1 The Candle/Box Problem

illustrates an issue which all learners experience. We get set on one way of doing something and it takes a conscious act to shift us out of this. We have to 'stop for a moment and think' about how else we might approach a problem. Indeed, when Duncker merely said 'Now think!' to his problem-solvers when they were stuck, he significantly increased the likelihood of their making the crucial breakthrough. If we simply carry on seeing the world in the same way as we always have, being merely creatures of habit, we are at risk of being stupid when the world changes. If we can reflect and become more strategic about how we might change our approach, then we are effectively more intelligent. (Incidentally it seems that functional fixedness is not innate but something we acquire with age and experience; compared with 7-year-olds, 5-year-olds are

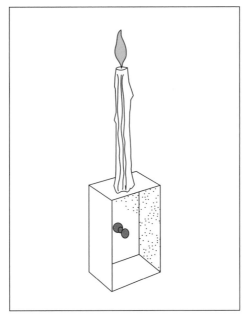

Figure 7.2 Solution to The Candle/Box Problem

smarter and more flexible, less inclined to suffer from functional fixedness.)[2]

It turns out that Edward Bear was right. If only he could have just stood back from what was going on he might have figured out a way of coming down the stairs without the affront to the frontal lobes of his brain.

In this chapter we will be looking at the ways in which people can become more intelligent by becoming more explicitly strategic about what they do. But we want to enter an important caveat right from the word go. While it is sometimes helpful to stop and think, it is also smart sometimes to keep going with what you are doing. Being strategic means knowing *when* to be reflective and when to go with the flow. Why? Because being strategic is hard work and

NEW KINDS OF SMART

demanding of our energies, and also because sometimes reflection turns into self-consciousness and gets in the way of smooth expertise. We mustn't fall into the trap of thinking that because reflection is sometimes really useful, therefore we should do it as much of the time as possible. To a large extent, the more we are able to respond to the world automatically, the better! This is essentially what we meant earlier, especially in Chapter 1, when we were talking about cultivating the most effective 'habits of mind' for learning. The philosopher Alfred North Whitehead articulated this beautifully:[3]

It is a profoundly erroneous truism, repeated by all copy-books and by eminent people when they are making speeches, that we should cultivate the habit of thinking of what we are doing.

The precise opposite is the case. Civilization advances by extending the number of important operations which we can perform *without* thinking about them. Operations of thought are like cavalry charges in a battle – they are strictly limited in number, they require fresh horses, and must only be made at decisive moments.

To live intelligently and effectively, we need to become non-consciously adept at a large number of complex activities rather than having constantly to stop and expend the kind of mental energies that require 'fresh horses' and lots of extra effort. But

> "To live intelligently and effectively, we need to become non-consciously adept at a large number of complex activities rather than having constantly to stop and expend the kind of mental energies that require 'fresh horses' and lots of extra effort. But there are also times when it is critical to be able to 'change gear', and make use of strategic reflection."

there are also times when it is critical to be able to 'change gear', and make use of strategic reflection. (Later in this chapter we will see how this kind of thinking can be applied to the issue of learning transfer.)

One more piece of context. What we are going to be exploring in this chapter is closely allied to words and phrases like 'meta-cognition', 'meta-learning' and 'learning how to learn'. The narrow old view of intelligence used to see conscious deliberate thought as essentially related to general cognitive ability. It could therefore be measured in tests of our skill at, for example, solving difficult puzzles. Perhaps because thinking, and for that matter learning, are largely invisible, there was little interest in what was going on beneath the surface, in the less conscious processes of learning. But on our richer view, intelligent people need to be smart at developing lots of intuitive expertise, *and* be able to take control of the processes of their own learning when they need to.

Since the 1980s, as we have seen, scientists have discovered that learning itself is learnable. People can develop techniques and strategies which will help them become more effective learners. Some of these strategies we can become adept at applying without thinking, but others need to be deployed consciously and appropriately when we are faced with certain challenges. Luckily, and perhaps not surprisingly, getting better at learning produces better performance in tests and examinations.

To get the feel for this balance, let's imagine two students. We'll call them Edward Bear and Christina Robin.

Edward is an affable boy who seems not to be fulfilling his potential. (Change the name and he can just as easily be a girl, of course.) When he remembers to do his homework, he normally plunges into whatever the task is without stopping to think how best he might approach it. In class he frequently runs out of time and hands in work which is incomplete. Once he has written something, he is loath to change it. He often gets stuck, finding himself unable to change tack once he has begun something in a certain way. Edward is a pretty good footballer but has recently been told by his teacher that he does not take practising seriously enough and that his place in the team may be under threat if he cannot be more focused and methodical. He does not enjoy being given feedback by his teacher or being asked to show his workings. In class, Edward just likes to get things done. Edward often feels like a bit-part actor in his own learning dramas, never quite understanding what is going on, so he is rarely able to do anything other than just act on the first impulse that comes to mind. His approach is over-whelmingly automatic, rarely stopping to take control of what he is doing.

Christina Robin (or Christopher if you prefer) is quite different. She surprises her parents and teachers alike with the degree of her reflectiveness and resourcefulness. She loves to chat to her friends to find out how they approach their homework and is often to be heard arranging to meet up with one of them to plan her work. In lessons and in life Christina seems to be clear about what she knows and where she needs to ask for help. Her MSN messages (and Tweets!) to friends are full of questions about how she might go about whatever she is interested in; her English book is full of many different drafts of the prose and poetry she has been asked to write with her own marginal comments much in evidence. This month Christina has two clear goals: to finish her history project and to go and watch a band (of Year 11 students) that she and her mates have heard are really good so that she can figure out how best to organize a set of songs for her own group. Christina relishes feedback, loving to think through the process of what she is doing. In Christina's head there is a constant stream of helpful talk going on. 'What am I being asked to do here?', 'Should I try this approach?', 'How am I getting on?', 'Have I got enough time for this?', 'Maybe I should try a different method', 'I think I'd better give up now and try something else', and so on.

Christina, in short, is able to regulate the pace and methods of her learning, where Edward has not. She is becoming increasingly reflective and is constantly developing her strategic intelligence.

Getting to grips with strategic intelligence

Schools are often not confident about the issues we want to raise in this chapter. For many years they focused too much on outputs and results rather than getting to grips with the *processes* going on inside learners' heads. In so far as more strategic approaches to learning have been used, they have tended to dwell on relatively superficial aspects of self-regulation such as study skills or more easily communicable elements such as revision planning or time management. In this chapter we will touch on some of the key processes which take place inside our heads as we learn more about learning. For the goal of effective schooling must surely be the cultivation of learners who are in charge of their own learning voyages, able to act as their own learning 'skippers' or 'navigators'. Learners need to be able to stand on the strategic bridge of their minds, as well as make use of the neural engine-room of learning, as they navigate their way through the learning waters they face.

> **"Learners need to be able to stand on the strategic bridge of their minds, as well as make use of the neural engine-room of learning, as they navigate their way through the learning waters they face."**

Meta-cognition and self-regulation

In tracing the history of strategic intelligence, it may be helpful to look a little more closely at these four concepts: meta-cognition/ meta-learning, self-regulation, reflection and transfer. *Meta-cognition*, for some, a daunting term, is essentially thinking about thinking, just as meta-learning is thinking about learning. Meta-cognitive skills are the higher order skills which ensure learners have the ability to stand back and take control of their own learning rather than, as in the case of Edward Bear, always having to be on 'automatic pilot'.

In 1979, developmental psychologist John Flavell[4] usefully identified three elements of metacognition which we list below with contemporary examples:

1 *Knowledge of self* (e.g. knowing that you concentrate more when you turn the iPod off).

2 *Knowledge of task* (e.g. knowing that working in a group involves consciously checking that everyone is on board).

3 *Knowledge of strategies* (e.g. knowing when it is smart to keep going and when you'd be better to go to bed and get a good night's rest).

Robert Sternberg, intelligence expert and creator of the concept of 'successful intelligence', has developed a theory that makes explicit links between intelligence and meta-cognition. As he puts it, meta-cognition is the executive process which people use for 'figuring out how to do a particular task or set of tasks, and then making sure that the task or set of tasks are done correctly'.[5] The good news is that learning to think about learning not only helps students become more effective learners, it also enhances performance on tests and in examinations, as Chris Watkins has shown,[6] and has been further explored in the work of the UK's Campaign for Learning[7] and in studies[8] in the UK, the USA and in Finland.

At the heart of meta-cognition is the second of the two terms we want to explore, *self-regulation*. Here the work of Dale Schunk and Barry Zimmerman is useful.[9] Zimmerman explains the idea like this:

> Students can be described as self-regulated to the degree that they are meta-cognitively, motivationally, and behaviourally active in their own learning process. Such students personally initiate and direct their own efforts to acquire knowledge and skill rather than relying on teachers, parents or other agents of instruction.[10]

Students who are self-regulated increasingly become their own teachers or, as we shall suggest later in this chapter, are able to summon up the 'coach in their head' as they are learning.

Paul Pintrich[11] has suggested a useful model of how self-regulation takes place in practice. Pintrich suggest that there are four phases in self-regulated learning that involve thinking, feelings, altering behaviour and reading any cues afforded by the context in which learning takes place. These are his four phases:

1 Forethought, planning and activation, e.g. goal-setting and goal-orientation, activating prior content knowledge.

> **"Students who are self-regulated increasingly become their own teachers or, . . . are able to summon up the 'coach in their head' as they are learning."**

2 Monitoring, e.g. awareness and self-observation.

3 Control, e.g. selection of appropriate strategies.

4 Reaction and reflection, e.g. with regard to nature of the task and its context.

In a development which parallels Carol Dweck's work on self-belief and expandable intelligence (see pages 33–4), Krista Muis[12] has suggested that as well as the four phases suggested by Pintrich, *epistemic beliefs* (what individuals believe about the nature of knowledge and knowing) play a key role in self-regulation. Just as Dweck has shown that it matters what you believe about how expandable intelligence is, so, Muis suggests, your beliefs about the type of knowledge required in any subject influence the degree to which you can regulate your learning in this context. So in mathematics, for example, where theorems and proofs are a key element of the epistemology of that subject, students whose own epistemic beliefs are similarly 'rational' tend to be more likely to use effective self-regulation strategies. Of course there is a danger of associating any one approach to knowledge with any specific subject (some of the greatest mathematical thinkers have combined high levels of empiricism and intuition in their approaches!), but once again, it is interesting to note the power of self-belief in any definition of intelligence.

Reflective practices

One of the most cited authorities in the general area of what we are calling strategic intelligence is Donald Schön.[13] Schön's theory of 'reflection-in-action' has been highly influential in the design of teaching practice for student teachers, and is widely used in the training of other professionals such as nurses and care workers. Reflection-in-action is essentially thinking on your feet. So, for example, when something unexpected happens you might express surprise, but then you might want to go back and check something out before you continue with a particular course of action. Or perhaps you might for a moment deliberately explore your puzzlement to see if it holds some clues as to what you might do next.

Schön contrasts reflection-in-action with 'reflection-on-action', essentially the off-line review function in learning (for example, mulling over why you did what you did after the event, and dreaming up 'better ways of handling the situation next time'). In both the classroom and other real-world contexts, learners can boost their strategic intelligence by getting better at reflection-in-action.

Understanding learning transfer

Some of the most powerful thinking in the area of strategic intelligence has come from David Perkins.[14] His work is particularly helpful in two crucial areas: defining what strategic (or reflective) intelligence actually is, and seeking to understand the mechanisms of 'transfer' that is, how something that had been learned in one context becomes available in a different setting. We think that transfer is a very important aspect of strategic intelligence. Intelligent people are good at expanding their repertoire of knowledge and skills, so they can meet new situations as well equipped as possible. But they also need to be able to bring the right bits of that knowledge and experience to bear on new situations. It is no use being really well informed if what you know does not come to mind at the appropriate moment – and that is where transfer comes in.

Perkins describes strategic intelligence in terms quite similar to Flavell's and Sternberg's. He sees it as 'a repertoire of beliefs and strategies about thinking and learning'. Perkins argues that there are basically three kinds of intelligence. The first he calls *neural intelligence*, which is essentially the innate 'envelope of ability' sometimes referred to as 'g' or general intelligence. The second he calls *experiential intelligence*, which is the vast body of knowledge and skills that people acquire in all the different contexts in which they grow up. Experiential includes doing experiments in science or learning to play in a rock band at home. If neural intelligence emphasizes more the 'nature' side of 'nature or nurture', experiential intelligence concentrates on the 'nurture' aspect.

For much of the time, says Perkins, we get on well enough using our neural and experiential intelligences, but every so often we need to call for a different kind of intelligence – the stand back and think kind – which he calls *reflective intelligence*. This encompasses all the tactics and strategies people use to make make the most of their neural and experiential intelligences. Reflective intelligence is pretty close to our idea of strategic intelligence: the 'cognitive cavalry charges' of the earlier Whitehead quotation. Reflective intelligence is especially important, says Perkins, 'in situations that require breaking set ways, unseating old assumptions, and exploring new ones'[15]. Standing back and invoking their mental control systems at a higher level is what strategically intelligent people do when they are gnawing away at intellectually demanding or emotionally complex tasks.

This aspect of our intelligence is largely a conscious function. We need to invoke it at key moments. You can think of it as the 'coach in your head'. It is as if you have a benign voice inside you that speaks up at just the right moment, reminding you of a different or better way of doing or thinking about something – but which is not yet 'second nature' to you. We say 'benign', but it is also possible for this 'coach' to be critical and undermining. It is one of the most important jobs of real coaches in life – parents and teachers, as well as sports coaches – to install in young people's heads the best on-board coaching voice they can. Our internal coach notices when something we are doing seems to be causing us anxiety and reminds us of times we have felt similarly and what we did that worked. Even though we may have committed considerable mental energy to something – the creation of a piece of drama, for example – our friendly coach sometimes asks us to have second thoughts, in this case, perhaps, causing to ponder whether we need be using a scripted approach when mime or improvisation might be more powerful. Our powerful inner coach is able to stand outside us as we learn and check whether:

- we have settled on a method too quickly;
- we have used all available resources to best effect;
- we are limiting our options through our chosen method, etc.

Being able to look at ourselves as we learn in a self-conscious way enables us to deploy our learning resources more strategically. It is also closely connected with our ability to transfer what we have learned from one context to another.

David Perkins is especially helpful here. With his colleague Gavriel Salomon he distinguishes between two kinds transfer, what they call 'low road' and 'high road'.[16] Low road transfer occurs when a new context spontaneously reminds you of an earlier experience. A good example would be the first use of a new mobile/cell phone. Although not identical to your last one, you easily transfer your knowledge of previous telephones and rapidly adjust to using your new one. A similar example would be driving a new car or even driving a small van when you are normally a car driver. The situation has enough clues and correspondences in it to prompt you to act in the right way. Your 'reading' of the new context is essentially a reflex reaction and largely non-conscious (although you may need to briefly stop to check your intuitive reactions).

High road transfer is different. It takes place when you more consciously seek to dredge up and apply things you have learned in contexts which may be quite different from the one you now find yourself in. Maybe you were taught to count to ten when you hurt yourself as a child (as a means of making it less likely that you would scream out in agony). Years later you find yourself sitting in a staff meeting and, infuriated by the wilful disagreeableness of a colleague, you are about to shout something rude at them when you become aware of the coach in your head 'prompting' you to try something you have not used for many a long year. After a moment's thought you quietly start counting to ten and, after doing so, you find that your anger has subsided sufficiently for you to concentrate on the issue at hand and ignore your irritating colleague. Your on-board coach has given you the *presence of mind* to save you from creating an embarrassing situation!

(This is also what friends are for! We have learned to check grumpy emails with each other before we send them to a third party – and will often remind each other of the longer-term negative consequences that might ensue. Sometimes the second-thoughts trigger is outside us – but it is very useful for our minds to have the capacity to do it by themselves as well.)

High road transfer requires you to have used your strategic

intelligence and extracted the essence of the learning – the learning 'juice' – from an earlier situation so that you can apply it. High road transfer involves two essential strategic learning skills: reflection and abstraction. In the previous case, the coach in your head has reflected that building in a short time-delay helps to defuse emotion and you have abstracted this into a rule of thumb 'count to ten'.

The distinction between low road and high road is much more than just a theoretical one as it has a direct influence on the way we teach in and beyond the classroom. Effective learners regularly use the low road method. They learn to do so by lots of varied practice in the original context so that they begin to recognize patterns and respond appropriately without having to think about it. The more difficult of the two – high road transfer – is a kind of cavalry charge (to go back to the quotation we used on page 134). It is mentally expensive and if we are in the flow of something, such mental interruptions can easily distract us. High road transfer is at the core of strategic intelligence. In practical terms it often takes the form of rules of thumb, thinking routines, instructions-to-self, good intentions, planning processes, heuristics, and so on.

To make it more likely that high road transfer will occur we need to do the following:

- practise in as many different contexts as possible (just as with low road transfer but even more important here);

- teach students how they might transfer what they are learning at the point when they first encounter it;

- cultivate the pattern-making disposition of students to look for connections in all of their learning, helping them to see what is similar, what is different.

We believe that schools are only just starting to understand the sophisticated processes involved in teaching students to get better at transferring their knowledge. Perkins has an amusing metaphor[17] to describe the common approaches associated with transfer. The first he calls the Bo Peep theory. Like the sheep in the nursery rhyme which find their way home wagging their tales behind them, the first fallacy is that transfer happens (or should happen) automatically as if by osmosis. Unfortunately the research suggests that it does not. The Bo Peep approach is wishful thinking. The second approach he calls the lost sheep theory in which teachers despair of being able to teach for transfer and simply concentrate on what is going on in their own classroom, accepting that much of what is learned will be lost along the way. The lost sheep theory is a counsel of despair as far as transfer is concerned. We, like Perkins, urge you all to adopt the third approach: become what he calls good shepherds, nurturing more strategically intelligent approaches in the ways we have described above.

Starting out

In the 1980s, schools first began to grapple with some of issues discussed in this chapter by teaching something which has become known as 'study skills'. For those about to take public examinations, these were often served up as part of a revision programme. For students who were less 'academic', whole courses were developed.

Later, in the 1990s, sometimes under the banner of 'thinking skills', schools began to teach useful problem-solving techniques directly – explaining to students about breaking problems into their constituent parts, how to make abstract ideas more concrete by drawing them as a picture, when to think aloud, and so on. The

Philosophy for Children[18] movement has also had a role in the development of sophisticated approaches to thinking, questioning and dialogue, often encouraging young children to develop big questions which they then take the responsibility of exploring.

So, too, has Assessment for Learning[19] (AfL), an approach to formative assessment which has spread from the UK throughout the world. An example of AfL would be the encouragement of students to put up their hands *when they want help* rather than when they want *to give an answer* (so inducing better self-regulation and resilience). Sometimes inspired by the work of the Campaign for Learning,[20] schools have introduced 'learning to learn' courses. These often contain useful tools and processes but evaluations often find that they count for little if they merely treat the processes of learning in isolation and are not reinforced in 'normal lessons' by all teachers all of the time. To be most effective, learning to learn needs to be taught as an integrated part of the subjects which make up the school curriculum and the culture.[21]

How teachers go about teaching – the roles they adopt – seems to be as important as their more deliberate planning, in developing strategic intelligence. David Leat and Mei Lin at Newcastle University,[22] drawing on extensive interviews with pupils, have helpfully summarized ten teacher roles which seem to help. We have chosen just three of these which seem particularly relevant, and included pupils' comments.

- *Collating ideas* – Teachers build a sense in pupils that they have a choice as to how they go about their learning. One student commented: 'She was making us look at other people's work to understand, to see what they were writing about.'

- *Making pupils explain themselves* – 'Instead of just letting us write down anything, she asked us why we wrote it down, why we thought it was a good idea . . . instead of just writing it down and saying that's right, like you've got to have a reason for thinking that's right.'

- *Making connections* – Teachers suggesting analogies and suggesting contexts where pupils might be able to apply their own learning.

Going deeper

Some well-researched and trialled tools have been developed into an approach called Visible Thinking as part of Harvard's Project Zero.[23] These routines do just as their name implies, making the processes of thinking and learning visible (and audible!). Students use and practise these routines in a number of different contexts and begin to internalize certain effective ways of 'surfacing' their learning.

A useful tool: Visible Thinking

CONNECT–EXTEND–CHALLENGE

1   How are the ideas and information connected to what you already know?

2   What new ideas did you get that extend your thinking in new directions?

3   What is still challenging or confusing for you? What questions or puzzles do you now have?

Guy has developed an approach to helping students expand their learning capacity, Building Learning Power (BLP), which we mentioned earlier. One of the tools that BLP makes use of is a series of quizzes that ask students every so often to reflect on the development of their own learning habits and attitudes. Available to students online (so they can take the quizzes at home), the program gives feedback, modelling the kinds of reflective thought processes that the on-board coach might make use of.[24]

To make use of the Tracking Learning Online tool, students answer Rarely, Sometimes, Often or Always to statements like these:

1 I stick at things even when they are hard.
2 It helps to understand if I put myself in other people's shoes.
3 I plan my learning carefully.
4 I can change tack when I'm learning if needs be.
5 I learn well as part of a team.
6 I try to link new things to what I know already.
7 I like thinking carefully and methodically.
8 I think about how I'm learning.
9 I can stick to what I believe in group discussions.
10 I use my imagination to explore possibilities.

Their responses can form the basis of discussions between students in class, or between student and teacher as part of periodic reviews of their development as learners. Such conversations seem to be really helpful in encouraging students to talk with greater precision about their own learning. They are a practical way of encouraging formative assessment which learners can use to influence their own choice of strategies.

For example, if the quiz reveals that students only rarely try to make links inside their heads – in other words, they are not yet well practised at high road transfer – teachers can construct opportunities and prompts for them to do this. As teachers and students get more confident in using these kinds of self-reports, a next logical step might be for them to develop the quiz by adding some of your own statements. (We suspect that one of the reasons why many approaches to 'meta-cognition' and 'learning to learn' have had disappointing results is because they do not *coach* the process very clearly, and do not offer students a rich language – as the quiz questions do – in which to think about their own learning habits and strategies.)

Ideas into practice

Developing strategic intelligence is complex and important work. But it can all too easily be undermined if teachers *advocate* some of the approaches we have described but retreat to more conventional chalk and talk approaches when the going gets tough.

To encourage learners to develop their strategic intelligence, it helps if you present learners with potential tools and approaches – 'scaffolding' in the language of Vygotsky – which you can then gradually remove so that learners are increasingly resourceful and self-reliant.

To help you think how you might try out ideas about strategic intelligence, you might like to wonder:

1 How can I create enough reflective space in a busy day so that I am not, like Edward Bear, constantly

bumping my head on the stair? How I can do this both with other colleagues and with learners in the classroom?

2 What thinking and learning routines do I already consciously make use of myself? Which do I find are the most helpful? How easily could I write them down clearly and reflect on them?

3 How can I help my students to become more strategic learners? How can I help them discover when it is smart to stay immersed in what they are doing, and when it is smarter to stand back and take stock? Could I design activities that would help them experiment with this?

4 How can I develop the 'coach in the head' idea so that students start to develop this kind of positive self-talk? What would that mean for the way I give feedback (specifically so that they can start to give themselves feedback when I am not around)?

5 Would it be a good idea to encourage group members to take it in turns to be the 'reflector' – someone who watches how the group is working and comments on what they notice from time to time?

6 How can I actively teach for transfer? How can I create more opportunities for students to practise their learning in different contexts? Could I muddle up activities more, so they have to think which skills to use, rather than assuming it is the ones they have most recently learned?

7 Could I get students to develop some simple statements about learning like the ones in Tracking Learning Online and then use them to monitor their own progress? How much help would I need to give them to get them going on such an activity? Which of my students are already the most articulate about their own learning, and how could I make best use of them?

8

Intelligence is Ethical

*Education organized around a reasonable number of
broad talents and interests, augmented and filled out by
serious inquiry into common human problems, stands the
best chance of achieving a meaningful equality. Such
education, in which students are active co-creators of
curriculum, is a truly liberal education for both personal
and public life in a democracy.*

Nel Noddings[1]

In a famous experiment[2] three groups of young children are given
an opportunity to play with a bobo doll (a large inflatable doll) in a
room which also has other toys to play with. Individual children
from each of the three groups enter the room and have markedly
different experiences. One group has an adult who verbally abuses
and attacks the doll with a mallet. One has an adult who is passive.
The third is a control group with no adult. The children are not
allowed to play at this stage. They are then taken into another room
with a similar selection of toys and a bobo doll. The children who

153

witness the adult being aggressive are themselves more aggressive when they are left to play. Perhaps not surprisingly aggression breeds aggression. We learn our behaviour from others. And children easily copy the behaviour of trusted adults around them.

Now stop and consider the experiences of much older students. In another piece of research[3] undergraduate theological students at Princeton University were invited to take part in a study about their ability to think quickly. The students were split into two groups. The first group were told that they will have to walk over to another building and give a talk to other students about employment opportunities for theological graduates, while the second group is led to believe that their task will be to talk about the parable of the Good Samaritan. In a further twist another variable was introduced. Three different levels of urgency were conveyed to them about the talk they had to give. The first were told that they were already late and must hurry, the second that they had just enough time to get to the hall and the third that they had a few extra minutes.

As the subjects walked over to the other building they passed a man slumped against a wall who was coughing and groaning and seemed to be in severe need of assistance. The results were stunning. Those who were going to be exploring the Good Samaritan story were no more likely to stop and help the distressed man (in reality an actor) than those who were going to talk about employment. It was those who were in a hurry who were less likely to stop. The Good Samaritan experiment (as it has become known) can be interpreted on many levels. Perhaps the most powerful message it leaves us with is that learning about good works does *not* necessarily change our behaviour. Believing something does not mean that you will necessarily put it into practice; the pressure of time is enough for knowledge and good intentions to be overwritten by expediency.

Getting to grips with ethical intelligence

In this chapter we will consider the last of our 'new kinds of smart', the ethical dimension of intelligence. We argue that true intelligence is not morally neutral. Hitler might have been cunning, even clever, but he was not intelligent in the deepest sense in which we would like to be able to use the word. For just as we made the case in a previous chapter for intelligence being a social phenomenon, so we also want to argue that it is also a matter of our goals and intentions.

Intelligence is what enables us to fulfil our needs and desires, and to avoid what is harmful or noxious. But what if we are confused about what we want and don't want? What if we think that some kinds of success make us happier than they really do, or that some misfortunes are actually not as bad as we fear them to be? Then our intelligence will be misdirected. Or, what if we underestimate the effect on ourselves of behaving callously or selfishly towards others? Then all our smart striving might end up damaging ourselves, as well as the vital 'web of social reciprocity' (as Jerome Bruner once put it) on which we depend.[4] And that would not be smart at all. We might run out of partners in the dance of life!

Thus the capacity to act in ways which help others – to be considerate and compassionate – might well turn out to be an aspect of what it is to be intelligent over time. If we are to cultivate the wholesome passions necessary for this, then we need to be able to distinguish between what are truer or deeper needs (as the real Good Samaritan did) as opposed to more selfish ego-driven ones (the perceived pressures of time, for example). To do this we need our intelligent compass to be sensitive to moral issues, as well as to our own fulfilment, and our lives to be based on an optimal balance between them.

In this chapter we will contrast 'good' intelligence with some more toxic or misguided behaviours. We will look at the way

> "The capacity to act in ways which help others – be considerate and compassionate – might we turn out to be an aspect of what it is to be intelligent over time."

in which our minds develop a sense of moral purpose and at the dilemmas which schools face when attempting to deal with this important but especially complex ethical dimension. And we will explore some ways in which schools may be able to cultivate the kinds of dispositions which are likely to sit well with ethically intelligent behaviour.

Some of the evidence suggests that, in these terms, things are pretty grim today for more than a few young people.[5] Surveys reveal that many children and young people, despite being materially comfortable, are unhappy, prone to self-harm and recklessness, obese, likely to drink alcohol to excess, depressed, isolated in front of a television or computer, unable to 'play' properly and perceived by adults to be likely to commit crimes. A major study in the UK undertaken by the Children's Society – The Good Childhood Inquiry[6] – pinpoints some of these trends: increasing material wealth (as characterized by ownership of mobile phones and the like) is set against increasing levels of anxiety; better education and health coexist with compulsive consumerism; greater tolerance of diversity and strong interests in environmental issues, for example, sit alongside excessive individualism. But of course the picture is not all doom and gloom. The same Inquiry reports that 87 per cent of children say that they are happy[7] and its authors constantly reaffirm a deep-rooted belief in the positive power of young people as a force for good. As well as showing the many positive attributes young people exhibit, other surveys[8] confirm the very mixed picture of child well-being even in economically developed countries.

The idea of moral psychology

As we write, US President Barack Obama has completed his first one hundred days in office. The moral tone from the leader of the world's superpower is changing. University of Virginia psychology professor Jonathan Haidt, perhaps sensing more receptive ears than those of the previous incumbent of this high office, has distilled a variety of recent research studies into some powerful advice for the incoming president, several strands of which will emerge throughout this chapter.[9]

First of all, Haidt identifies five important moral senses or concerns that he claims run deep in all human societies. They are:

1 Aversion to and protection from harm.

2 Fairness.

3 Loyalty to the group.

4 Respect for authority.

5 Not defiling one's 'spiritual purity'.

The first two of these, concerning harm (for example, our understanding of concepts like sympathy, nurturing and well-being) and fairness (including our anger at injustice), Haidt argues, are well researched and widely discussed. They are values that we all hold dear. But the next three are more politically loaded. They are valued more highly by some social groups than others. Some of the conflicts within societies, says Haidt, reflect this difference in prioritization. Broadly, political conservatives place greater emphasis on the last three, even when they might infringe to some extent on the first two, while those of a more liberal persuasion are more likely to baulk at any such infringement. For them, protection of the weak and a deep sense of fairness trump patriotism and deference to authority, for example. It is not that either side consists of 'bad people'; it is that their moral priorities stack up differently, so when different 'goods' conflict, they behave differently.

Haidt suggests that, if Obama is to carry the whole USA with him, he will need to expand his moral vocabulary to ensure that the liberals who swept him to power can at least acknowledge the moral validity of loyalty to the group, authority, and concerns about 'spiritual purity' and develop more progressive positions on each of them. As the first African-American president, he is, for example, well placed to develop a more delicate balance between traditionally liberal concerns with diversity and social inclusion, and traditionally right-wing concerns with economic justice and fairness. Haidt argues that such a balance may command a wider social consensus and appeal.

Elsewhere,[10] Haidt traces the history of the field known as moral psychology. His own definition of moral systems is particularly helpful:

> Moral systems are interlocking sets of values, practices, institutions, and evolved psychological mechanisms that work together to suppress or regulate selfishness and make social life possible.

In this chapter we will be exploring some of the ways in which we can become more ethical by regulating our selfishness and so expand the boundaries of our real-world intelligence.

Intelligence, we think, is ultimately about pursuing our passions and goals in life in a way that is compatible with the well-being of our fellow men and women. And this is the specifically ethical dimension we are exploring in this chapter. Charles Handy has a nice phrase to describe such a disposition; he calls it 'proper selfishness'.[11] He says:

> Life surely is the chance to make the best of ourselves. We owe it to everybody to give them that chance, even if they make a mess of it. We can detect in each of us a tendency towards good and the opposite tendency towards evil.

> "Intelligence, we think, is ultimately about pursuing our passions and goals in life in a way that is compatible with the well-being of our fellow men and women."

> "Life surely is the chance to make the best of ourselves. We owe it to everybody to give them that chance, even if they make a mess of it."
> Charles Handy

The stages of moral development

One of the most detailed descriptions of our moral development is to be found in the work of Lawrence Kohlberg.[12] Building on Piaget's work, Kohlberg charts six stages of moral development which he arranges into three levels. There is not space here to explore these in detail but it is worth describing the progression he envisages. The five moral concerns that Haidt identifies are shaped and moulded as children grow up. (For example, we all know that 'It's not FAIR!' is a powerful cry in childhood, as they learn, sometimes painfully, how their particular society interprets fairness, and how other moral values, such as respect for authority, come into conflict.)

Initially children learn simple rules (it's bad to steal) and connect breaking these with punishment. Then they begin to realize that the interpretation of a rule may also involve different viewpoints (what looks like someone hurting someone else may be an act of self-defence). Gradually they move in to more subtle territory as they realize that the moral sense is not an abstract world of right and wrong but a dynamic set of interpersonal relationships. This involves the development of good motives and feelings for others such as love, empathy, trust, and concern. From this they grasp a bigger picture, that moral development is about maintaining the social order. Societies need rules and, even if we have a good reason and strong and genuine feelings, we are still subject to those rules. (As adults we may still have to pay a fine even if we jump a red traffic light on a dash to the maternity hospital with a woman about to give birth.) And finally Kohlberg acknowledges stages that go beyond conventional morality and imagines individuals asking such fundamental questions as 'What makes for a good society?' In a moral world, there have to be ways of changing unjust rules and assumptions, for example, that women cannot vote, or that animals have no rights.

The challenge, for both parents and schools, is how, if we accept this broad progression, we create educational environments in which children will progress through these stages. How will we encourage children to think these complex issues through and then act accordingly? Though UK and some other schools are obliged by law to attend to the 'moral and spiritual development' of their pupils, in practice the pressures on them force many to focus almost exclusively on the business of doing successful schooling in terms of examinations, curricula, league tables and so forth.

Adopting a perspective from positive psychology (which focuses on the development of personal strengths rather than the regulation of weaknesses), Christopher Peterson and Martin Seligman,[13] along with some of the world's most eminent thinkers in this area, have attempted to create a framework of what they call 'character strengths and virtues'. The framework seeks to provide teachers and other educators with a series of research-based areas on which to focus as they educate young people.

After an extensive trawl of highly diverse cross-cultural literatures, they have identified 24 strengths which are grouped around six virtues (see Table 8.1). Peterson and Seligman talk of their work as the 'science of human strengths' and in this are getting very close to what we understand by 'ethical intelligence'.

They start with virtues, the core characteristics which moral philosophers and religious leaders over the centuries have promoted. But their focus is not on the moral elements which make up these virtues (which could have led them to moralize), so much as on the psychological ingredients (processes or mechanisms) that underpin the virtues.

They suggest that cultivating the strengths listed in Table 8.1 is at the heart of the agenda we face in education today.

In a book written jointly with Howard Gardner and Anna Craft, Guy has tried to link the idea of ethical and moral behaviour with the slippery concepts of 'wisdom' and 'creativity'.[14] He suggests that a core disposition underlying fairness, for example, might well be the human capacity for empathy, and wonders whether the dynamic exploration of the motivations of young people's and adults' heroes and heroines in schools might be one practical way of exploring

Table 8.1 Psychological ingredients underpinning the virtues

Character virtues	*Character strengths*
Wisdom and Knowledge	Creativity Curiosity Open-mindedness Love of learning Perspective
Courage	Bravery Persistence Integrity Vitality
Humanity	Love Kindness Social intelligence
Justice	Citizenship Fairness Leadership
Temperance	Forgiveness and mercy Humility and modesty Prudence Self-regulation
Transcendence	Appreciation of beauty and excellence Gratitude Hope Humour Spirituality

ethical intelligence in action. 'It could be that the ability to adopt a kind, wise, and disinterested perspective itself grows out of the development of empathy.' The more you master the ability to look at the world through the eyes of an increasing range of other people, the more it becomes possible to learn greater relative objectivity, and to become more skilful at looking for ways of enhancing 'the good of all', rather than just 'me and my friends'.

> "The more you master the ability to look at the world through the eyes of an increasing range of other people, the more it becomes possible to learn greater relative objectivity, and to become more skilful at looking for ways of enhancing 'the good of all', rather than just 'me and my friends'."

Cultivating ethical intelligence in schools

Ethical or moral education has always been part of education. Long ago, Benjamin Franklin stated that: 'Nothing is of more importance for the public weal, than to form and train up youth in wisdom and virtue.' Schools have always had to declare their rules and sometimes their beliefs. Moral education in its broadest sense is one of the oldest topics of the school curriculum. In one sense, you cannot *not* teach ethics. Every school will have both an explicit curriculum and a hidden one, where the underlying messages about what is really valued are embodied in the everyday sense of 'how we do things round here'. Students often deduce the values of any institution more from the way teachers and other adults behave and from the way schools actually treat them than from any published statements of belief.[15]

Howard Gardner suggested that there is such a thing as an 'ethical mind', and that it is part of school's job to cultivate it.[16] We agree with him. Gardner sees the core features of ethical activity as striving to do what he calls 'good work' and trying to be a good citizen. He has embarked on a long-term study, through the Good Work Foundation, of what ethical actions actually look like in practice in the twenty-first century. Through interviews with a large range of professionals, he is beginning to tease out some generalizable principles.

Schools have a primary role in cultivating ethical minds. But like any endeavour that dares to use the word 'good', the process is not straightforward. Talking about 'good' inevitably courts accusations that someone is trying to impose their subjective morality onto someone else. But in education we simply cannot avoid it – education is, indelibly, a moral enterprise, as we have said. But Gardner suggests that the linguistic ambiguity of the word can be useful:

> Educators can smooth the road to an ethical mind by drawing attention to the other connotations of goodness. Students need to understand why they are learning what they are learning and how the knowledge can be put to constructive use.

Gardner has suggested four tests – the 4Ms – which he uses as indicators of good work:

1 *Mission*. The degree to which goals are explicitly articulated so that a sense of direction is clear.

2 *Models*. Exposure to individuals who embody good work and who can act as role models.

3 *Mirror-test (individual)*. The idea of regularly employing strategic intelligence to 'look in the mirror' and asking whether what is being done is being done ethically.

4 *Mirror-test (professional responsibility)*. The obligation to monitor and mentor others to develop good work.

If these are useful signposts along the way to promoting the development of ethical intelligence, the crucial question is, of course, how it can be done.

The two examples of research with which we started this chapter suggest two possibilities. From the bobo doll experiment we can remind ourselves – as Gardner does – of the enormously powerful influence of adult role models on the moral behaviour of children. And from the Good Samaritan we have the salutary lesson that learning about good behaviour does not necessarily mean that we start to *do* good works in our lives. Talking about moral issues may be helpful in instilling moral clarity and direction – or it may not. (For every young person who is inspired by a moral message, there may well be another who objects to being 'preached at', and is determined to spite the preacher by doing the exact opposite!)

In this context, Stanford's Nel Noddings makes a useful distinction between 'caring for' and 'caring about'.[17] She makes a compelling case that, for ethical intelligence to mean anything in practice, we need to do more than care *about* others in the abstract; we need to care *for* them in practical ways too. Interestingly we first learn about caring for, by experiencing it at first hand in the homes where we grow up, and then extrapolate that to learning how to care for others. Caring *about* wider issues such as 'the environment', 'justice' or 'poverty' is a more sophisticated achievement that involves thinking and reflection, and tends only to emerge later on in adolescence. And if it involves only an intellectual commitment, and does not result in practical and compassionate acts, Noddings argues that morality has lost its way.

The key, central to care theory, is this: caring-about (or perhaps a sense of justice) must be seen as instrumental in establishing the conditions in which caring-for can flourish ... Caring-about is empty if it does not culminate in caring relations.

Starting out

The simplest expression of ethical intelligence in schools involves explicit attempts to develop 'character' in young people. Across the world there are many examples of schools which through assemblies and lessons seek to do just this. Moral dilemmas are discussed and moral precepts are dispensed, sometimes within an explicitly religious framework, sometimes not. The problem with this is, that as we saw in the Good Samaritan experiment, while the moral compass may be there for all to see, there is no guarantee that it will be used or applied. And, as we were suggesting earlier in relation to Jonathan Haidt's advice to President Obama, the moral compass can also be heavily politicized.

The attempt to develop 'caring for' and 'caring about' is often seen in the way schools set up the familiar student council. Typically each class elects one or more representatives who meet, with varying degrees of autonomy and power, as a kind of mini-parliament. Sometimes such groups function really well, providing real opportunities for young people to debate moral issues and take practical action. Other times they are reduced to discussing technical issues such as the state of the toilets or the vending machines, or merely responding to an agenda received from their teachers. An effective student council is likely to be developing its own agenda, undertaking its own enquiries, taking an active role in shaping the ethical stance of the school, providing feedback to teachers on their teaching, shadowing members of staff to learn more about their roles, and so on. The kinds of approaches which might be used are likely to draw on those used in Philosophy for Children or Open Space (see pp. 147 and 125).

In many countries, junior versions of democratic participation go under the banner of 'citizenship education'. At its purest this involves enabling young people to make their own decisions and to take responsibility for their own lives, at school, at home and in their communities. As Bernard Crick put it:

> Citizenship is more than a subject. If taught well and tailored to local needs, its skills and values will enhance democratic life for all of us, both rights and responsibilities, beginning in school and radiating out.[18]

The challenge of citizenship education is the risk of nationalism and the difficulty of creating a neutral enough space for difficult conversations to be had.

A parallel approach is often referred to as 'character education'. The Character Education Partnership[19] in the USA has developed a useful self-analysis tool using the eleven headings in the box.

A useful tool: eleven principles of character education

1 Promotes core ethical values and supportive per-formance values as the foundation of good character.

2 Defines 'character' comprehensively to include think-ing, feeling and behaviour.

3 Uses a comprehensive, intentional and proactive approach to character development.

4 Creates a caring school community.

---

5 Provides students with opportunities for moral education.

6 Includes a meaningful and challenging academic curriculum that respects all learners, develops their character and helps them to succeed.

7 Strives to foster students' self-motivation.

8 Engages the school staff as a learning and moral community that shares responsibility for character education and attempts to adhere to the same core values that guide the education for students.

9 Fosters shared moral leadership and long-range support of the character education initiative.

10 Engages families and community members as partners in the character-building effort.

11 Assesses the character of the school, the school's staff functioning as character educators and the extent to which students manifest good character.

One aspect of education which is increasingly being tried out, especially in the USA, is service learning. Service learning integrates meaningful community service with teaching, learning and reflection. Often it involves voluntary work outside school and interaction with adults from a whole range of service-orientated organizations and professions. It is often called things like 'Voluntary service', 'Community curriculum' and 'Community activities'. In the UK this kind of activity is a core element of the Duke of Edinburgh's Award Scheme and there are similar programmes across the world designed to enrich the learning experience, nurture initiative, teach civic responsibility, and strengthen communities. Interestingly some research even suggests that that certain kinds of service learning, as well as enhancing students' social responsibility and ethical intelligence, may also have a positive impact on academic success.[20]

Each of the approaches listed above has something to commend it. The real challenge is to make the ethical dimension integral to the educational process or it can all too easily appear to be an add-on.

Going deeper

One of the best-known examples of schools which have deliberately set out to develop ethical intelligence is to be found in the city of Reggio Emilia in Italy. Here, in the aftermath of the Second World War, a community, appalled by its own passivity and complicity in the face of brutality, determined to raise future generations who would be morally stronger. It focused on laying the foundations for this kind of character in early years education. Reggio Emilia schools are explicitly trying to create ethically intelligent communities. Parents are seen as integral partners with teachers in the way that pre-schools are run. Learning is largely project- and enquiry-based and multiple points of view – the breeding ground for empathy, as we discussed earlier – are encouraged through what the schools call the 'One hundred languages of childhood' approach. ('Language' here includes the whole gamut of ways of interacting and communicating, including drawing, painting, playing, acting, and so on.)

Schools which are serious about cultivating the ethical dimensions seem to us to be explicitly encouraging flexibility, empathy, critical evaluation and creativity (especially the exploration of non-obvious solutions to real, difficult problems). Above all, they are acutely aware of the cultural dimension of school, of how the adults within them are powerful role models for good or ill. Reggio Emilia seems to have been so successful because it has put ethical and cooperative behaviour at the heart of its culture. Parents, teachers and students all genuinely share and listen to each other. Their patterns of thinking and acting are bound by the strong ethical sense that there must never again be a breakdown of democratic processes such as is evidenced by war.

Nel Noddings has useful things to suggest here about the four key processes involved in embedding the ethical approach:

1   *Modelling.* Teachers and others living their values.

2   *Dialogue.* Opportunities for debate, critique, evaluation and feedback.

3   *Practice.* Explicit opportunities for students to practise.

4   *Confirmation.* Trust, consistency and continuity and the absence of slogans.

There are clear links to Gardner's 4Ms here. As well as emphasizing the kinds of processes which seem to work, Noddings also urges us to be unapologetic in making the development of a caring ethical dimension of education one of our explicit moral purposes. She encourages educators to relax their impulse to control schools, encouraging instead what she calls 'responsible experimentation' in which more genuine autonomy is devolved to schools and within schools.

In Australia there has been a deliberate attempt to learn more about the development of ethical intelligence. Called the National Framework for Values Education in Australian Schools, its core idea is that:

placing values at the centre of the school and subsequently striving to live those values within the school community, produces children who are highly ethical and care for those in their lives, in their local community and for the global community and environment as well.[21]

Three years ago Guy was at a conference in Australia, held at Melbourne's Glen Waverley Secondary College. In the afternoon, a group of visitors watched some presentations by students on their 'extended enquiry' projects. In Year 9 at Glen Waverley, students have the opportunity to spend every Friday of one semester working in a small group on a project of their own devising. One of the presentations was by three girls, Surabhi, Stephanie and Fiona. They had been investigating detention centres for refugees and asylum seekers. Having seen such centres on the news, the girls were curious why they seemed to be uniformly so ugly and inhospitable. They read reports, interviewed some people who had spent months in these places, and created a sophisticated 10-minute PowerPoint presentation to display their findings.

They were not especially high-achieving students, but they spoke with great eloquence and passion about their research. And they explained to us that they were going to carry on their study, but that their question had shifted and sharpened. Now what they wanted to know was, as Surabhi put it, 'why Australians feel the need to behave so unkindly towards desperate strangers'. Their seriousness moved and inspired everyone in that room. And they told us that the project had greatly expanded their self-confidence, as well as their skills of researching, interviewing, collaboration and presentation. But they would not have had such an invaluable opportunity to stretch and strengthen their learning muscles in most schools. It was only because their school had a broader vision of education, and a degree of trust in young people, that they had been given the chance.

It turns out that the girls had later sent a DVD of their presentation to John Howard, then the Australian Prime Minister. They didn't get a reply. But their teacher, Adele Briskman, also encouraged them to submit their research to an international conference on human rights which was held in Melbourne in February 2007. Their submission was accepted, and very well received by the delegates. The experience was nerve-wracking – but having done it, the girls were delighted and very proud of themselves. More importantly, they became more ethically intelligent learners as a result. That's real education. It clearly isn't impossible to organize a school so that all young people get such opportunities.

Ideas into practice

In many ways this chapter contains ideas which are both fundamental to what intelligent schooling should be about but which are also extremely challenging to put into practice in schools.

To help you think how you might try out ideas about ethical intelligence, you might like to wonder:

1 How could I involve students more in real moral dilemmas so that they can learn more about how to approach these? Is it appropriate to get them to work with the real moral issues they grapple with out of school? And if so, what would be the best way?

2 What am I already doing in my own teaching to promote ethical intelligence? How do my own values influence who I am as a teacher? If I stand back, what values do I regularly *embody* (as opposed to the ones I regularly *profess*)?

3 How might I use Gardner's 4Ms in practice? Specifically who do I know or know of who embodies 'good work'? Could I bring them, or their example, more into my lessons?

4 How could I work with colleagues to think about how to create real opportunities for students to develop their ethical intelligence both in the classroom and outside it? It can be a delicate issue: how best to approach it?

5 How might the staff as a whole become more visible role models of people trying their best to wrestle with genuine ethical difficulties? Do we do enough to bring students into the complicated decision-making processes of the school?

6 Is it appropriate to challenge selfishness and materialism in schools, and, if so, how might we do this? Could we use our concern with climate change and sustainability to begin to look at these underlying issues more deeply?

7 Could I use the 'eleven principles' tool to suggest ways of taking stock of what my school is already doing in the area of ethical intelligence? How could I use it as the basis for a Professional Development session with colleagues?

9

Finale

It is increasingly evident that the educational methods we have been using for the past 70 years no longer suffice. They are based on scientific assumptions about the nature of knowledge, the learning process, and the different aptitudes for learning that have been eclipsed by new discoveries.

Lauren Resnick[1]

Let's begin this finale by rounding up and restating some of the themes that the 'orchestra' has been playing throughout the preceding chapters. When we have done that, we'll finish with some thoughts about where these ideas might lead in the future, and how they might become stronger and more differentiated. As we have said, the emerging science of learnable intelligence is a work-in-progress, and there are many questions left to explore, and even some wrong turnings – some of which we may have taken in this book – that may need to be retraced and rethought.

In the Prelude, we argued that schools are built on assumptions

174

about what kinds of people, with what kinds of minds, society needs. But they also rely on ideas about what 'minds' *are*: what aspects of children's minds are malleable and what are pre-determined, and how the malleable bits are shaped. As our understanding of the nature of learning and intelligence changes and develops, so too will the way lessons are organized, examinations are designed, curricula are specified, and teachers teach. In this book, we have tried to show how traditional views of intelligence are changing, and how those changes are impacting on schools – and might impact even more.

Expanding horizons

Intelligence is expanding, in two senses. First, our *conception* of what it means to be intelligent is expanding. Being smart does not just mean being able to solve abstract mathematical and verbal puzzles against the clock. The research tells us that this ability has little to do with how people go about dealing with tricky stuff in their everyday work, family and leisure lives. Nor does real-world intelligence depend on being good at *Trivial Pursuit*. Having a memory that is well stocked with free-floating 'facts', and being able to pull them out fast, on demand, does not seem to relate much to the wider issue of what it takes to live well in the twenty-first century.

Real-world intelligence has to do with how people respond to challenges that matter to them. As Jean Piaget said, being smart is not 'knowing lots';[2] it is how you think, feel and behave at the moments when your accumulated store of knowledge and skill *doesn't* give you a ready answer, and you have to 'think on your feet'. You may have a high IQ, you may even be a winner of

175

> "If education finds itself geared towards producing quiz-show contestants and professors of philosophy, and making people who turn out not to be good at ~~or interested in those~~ accomplishments feel second-rate, we think it has lost its way. Education itself has become a trivial pursuit."

> "Far from being a single commodity, we now know that 'intelligence' is a portmanteau name for something that is made up of many 'instruments', intricately orchestrated together to make harmonious 'music'."

Mastermind, but if at that moment of uncertainty and indecision you become paralysed and defensive, we don't think you can claim to be all that smart. If education finds itself geared towards producing quiz-show contestants and professors of philosophy, and making people who turn out not to be good at or interested in those accomplishments feel second-rate, we think it has lost its way. Education itself has become a trivial pursuit.

Intelligence is composite

Far from being a single commodity, we now know that 'intelligence' is a portmanteau name for something that is made up of many 'instruments', intricately orchestrated together to make harmonious 'music'. Being able to cope well with difficulty and uncertainty depends on self-discipline and perseverance. It depends on being on the look-out for sources of help, both material and social. It depends on the ability to attend carefully and concentrate strongly; and on the willingness to tinker, experiment and improve through well-designed practice. It requires imagination, intuition and empathy, as well as logic and criticism. It benefits from open-mindedness and non-defensiveness. In Chapter 1, we looked at several of the frameworks that have been developed to describe this composite nature of intelligence.

The second sense in which 'intelligence is expanding' refers not to the concept of intelligence, but to intelligence itself. There is abundant evidence that the real-world kind of intelligence (with which education should be concerned) is itself substantially expandable. It is not only more accurate, but educationally more productive, to be focusing on those aspects of mind which are capable of being developed. Put baldly: kids can get smarter, and it is school's job to help them. Approaches like Art Costa and Bena Kallick's *Habits of Mind*[3] or Guy Claxton's *Building Learning Power*[4] have developed hundreds of practical ways in which resilience, imagination, concentration and the rest can be stretched and strengthened in the course of 'normal lessons'.

> 66Put baldly: kids can get smarter, and it is school's job to help them.99

Intelligence is expandable

We explored this idea, and the evidence for it, in more detail in Chapter 2. We saw that the old attempt to split intelligence into the 'innate bit' and the 'learned bit' no longer holds water. Genes may specify an 'envelope of potential' for any one of us, but those envelopes are large, and where our intelligence ends up depends hugely on the experience, the encouragement and the guidance we have had. Of more significance is the finding that people's intelligence tends to be capped not so much by their genetic

> 66People's intelligence tends to be capped not so much by their genetic inheritance as by the acquired belief that it is fixed.99

inheritance as by the acquired belief that it is fixed. While this belief goes unarticulated and unchallenged, it leads students to imagine that, if they were 'bright' they would find learning easy, and so, when they have to struggle and persist, they feel stupid and helpless. And this misconception puts them off learning and trying. However, when teachers are able to bring this assumption to light, and give students the evidence to challenge it, many of them (though not all) are able to free up their learning again quite quickly. If schools are to help young people develop their real-world intelligence, the very least they can do is make sure they are not perpetuating the dysfunctional old view of 'fixed ability'.

Intelligence is practical

The narrow view of intelligence saw it not only as relatively fixed, but as abstract. This association between intelligence and abstract reasoning goes back a long way in our culture, and it runs deep. From Plato through the early Christian Fathers (and Mothers) to Descartes and on to the present day, the workings of the physical body have been seen as lowly, wild and untrustworthy compared with the higher, more civilized and more ethereal world of the intellect. But with the rise of modern neuroscience, as we saw in Chapter 3, we now know just how clever the physical body (and especially its brain) actually are – and we also know just how easy it is for the rarefied intellect to come up with very impractical and short-sighted ideas! Real-world intelligence involves 'walking the talk', as well as looking good on paper. The proof of the smart pudding is in the practical eating.

And physical activity – sketching, crafting, doodling and gesturing – turns out to be deeply involved in intelligent thinking and creating. Making and fixing things are *cognitively* sophisticated activities, not just bodily ones. Good footballers learn how to put themselves in an opponent's boots, and chefs need to think carefully about their menus. It does us no good, as a society, if we associate 'intelligence' with writing and reckoning, but not with dancing, gardening and plumbing. We need to expand our idea of intelligence to include hands and feet as well as ears and thoughts, and to organize schools so that the thousands of practical ways of being smart are as much valued as the tightly-argued case and the well-proven theorem. If people who are good at practical things feel their interests and skills mark them out as less 'bright', it is not just them who suffer. Societies need their makers and doers as much as (if not more than) their lawyers and professors.

> "Societies need their makers and doers as much as (if not more than) their lawyers and professors."

Intelligence is intuitive

Intelligence isn't only verbal, and sometimes it isn't even very conscious. Thinking carefully and logically is a part of being intelligent; but logic is often at its smartest when it is working in concert with less clear-cut forms of cognition. In Chapter 4 we saw that many highly creative people deliberately interweave periods of hard thinking with periods of not thinking about much at all. It looks as if the brain (and the body it is part of) are the true 'brains' behind our intelligence. And the brain speaks to consciousness in a whole variety of voices. Sometimes it speaks in well-formed sentences and arguments. Sometimes it speaks in images, dreams or even 'visions'. Sometimes it speaks in sudden flashes of insight, and sometimes in quiet inklings and promptings. Sometimes it speaks in premonitions or feelings of being touched or moved (for no apparent reason). And sometimes it speaks directly in actions and impulses, without any preceding or accompanying conscious experience at all.

There isn't just one best way of 'being intelligent': the smart brain seems to be designed to work in a wide range of complementary rhythms and registers. So schools should understand and acknowledge that, and make a place for the different types and tempi of intelligent activity. Creativity can't be reduced to an occasional frenzy of dancing and painting: it is too important for that. We saw how some schools are creating environments where children are encouraged to learn when and how to use different ways of thinking, while others are deliberately helping students learn how to 'think at the edge' of their current understanding, and to get better at heeding their more embodied kinds of knowing.

> "Creativity can't be reduced to an occasional frenzy of dancing and painting: it is too important for that."

Intelligence is distributed

You can't even tie intelligence down to what is going on in an individual person. The old view saw intelligence as a personal possession, but we saw in Chapter 5 that this is only half the story. Just as we have to acknowledge what is going on in the body and brain – at what philosophers call the 'sub-personal level' – as well as what is occurring in the conscious mind, so intelligence also depends on our being hooked up to what is going on outside the body, at the 'supra-personal level'. Human beings have evolved to be incredible tool-makers, tool-finders and tool-users. Just as a computer becomes more powerful when it is hooked up to a range of peripherals – zip-drives, modems, printers, webcams, and so on – so we amplify our own intelligence through the skilful use of a bewildering variety of artefacts. From telephones to tape measures, slide rules to spectacles, wall-charts to the worldwide web, real-world intelligence almost always depends on what David Perkins called 'person-plus'.

If schools are preparing young people to be their smartest in the real world, they need to respect and strengthen this basic tool-mindedness. Students can be helped to develop the disposition of resourcefulness – being on the look-out for smart ways of amplifying their own learning power – or they can be trained to think of this aspect of intelligence as 'cheating', and to respect only problem-solving that can be done 'all in the head' (or at least only with the assistance of a pad of paper and a ball-point pen).

But they also need help to look on tools as genuine amplifiers, to be used thoughtfully and with discernment, rather than as cognitive crutches that leave them helpless in a power cut. Person and tool need to work together in a way that makes an intelligent unit that is greater than the sum of the parts (not one where the person becomes lazy, dependent or mindless) – and this takes some smart coaching from teachers and parents. New tools (such as the internet) extend our resources; but they also bring with them new hazards and demand the development of new skills. Intelligent use of the internet requires strong discipline, focus and discrimination in the selection and evaluation of information. Smart surfers need to have developed the

> "Smart surfers need to have developed the disposition of intelligent scepticism, and a repertoire of methods for assaying knowledge claims."

disposition of intelligent scepticism, and a repertoire of methods for assaying knowledge claims.

Intelligence is social

The most powerful supra-personal resources are, of course, other people. Crowds are liable to 'group-think', and may behave in ways that are more hysterical or stupid than any of their individual members. But it is also true that two or three heads are often better than one, and that (as we tire of hearing at award ceremonies) no one individual could have 'done it' without a whole team of others. Intelligence is often more a collective accomplishment than an act of individual brilliance. And again, as with the use of material tools, the social dimension on intelligence is not something we have to persuade people of; it seems to be built in to our evolutionary make-up.

> "Intelligence is often more a collective accomplishment than an act of individual brilliance."

But just because our capacity for social intelligence is (in some sense) natural, that does not mean that we are all equally good at making use of it. As we saw in Chapter 6, individuals need to have certain skills, and groups need to have conducive attitudes and ways of working, if they are to be as smart as they can be. It is no use making people work or explore together if they are a bunch of closed-minded bigots, nor if they are all convinced that their way is 'obviously' the best, and all the others just have to 'be reasonable'. A well-functioning team is a super-charged problem-solving unit – but it needs skill and maintenance to get to that point and stay there. And team styles and methods need to be flexible, and members may need to be able to play different roles at different times. So schools should be concerned about much more than 'playing nicely' and 'waiting your turn': there is a whole social curriculum that needs addressing not through work-sheets about 'self-esteem' but through a rich and varied diet of learning opportunities, and enough (but not too much) explicit attention to how groups are functioning, and how individuals are growing in their ability to both create good teams, and to benefit from them.

Intelligence is strategic

The idea of explicitly reflecting on how a group is working brings us to the next expansion of intelligence, the one we considered in Chapter 7. This is the ability to stand back and take stock of things, to consider different options, and to change tack if it seems appropriate. This kind of strategic or reflective intelligence is not the same as the disciplined, logical thinking that sat at the centre of the old model of intelligence. In that model, analytical reasoning was supposed to be the best approach to difficulty. All you had to do was do it. But in the richer model we are presenting here, there are always several options about how to use your mind (+ brain + body + tools + companions) to the best advantage. Your default way of thinking or exploring might be the most powerful and appropriate approach – or it might not. You may know of a better way, but it is not the one that you load and run automatically. So real-world intelligence needs to be able to stop itself at the right moment, go 'off-line' and say, 'Hang on a minute. How's it going? What else might I try?'

Strategic intelligence enables you to be self-coaching and self-correcting: to make the best use of all your accumulated knowledge and experience, including what you might have been told, overheard or watched. Like other animals, we are creatures of habit; but unlike them we have the powerful potential to over-ride habit and try out new or less familiar ways of operating. We can transfer ideas from one context to another, and thus make the most of what we know. And this boosts our intelligence enormously – but, as before, only if we are 'minded' to make use of it. We have to develop the disposition to be self-interrupting and reflective – and that is what teachers should be helping

> "Strategic intelligence enables you to be self-coaching and self-correcting: to make the best use of all your accumulated knowledge and experience, including what you might have been told, overheard or watched."

students to do. Like any good coach, they should be explaining and modelling the reflective stance, providing plentiful opportunities for students to get stuck and change tack, and fading away the scaffolding of prompts and signposts, so the habit of considering alternative view-points and approaches gradually becomes second nature.

Intelligence is ethical

And finally, in Chapter 8, we considered a deeper facet of real-world intelligence – one that makes us think not just about intelligence but about wisdom. To be truly intelligent, it is not enough just to meet your challenges and pursue your interests as skilfully as you can: you need to be clear about what your deepest interests really are. You need to be able to see the big picture; to balance and resolve what is sometimes a bewildering portfolio of competing and conflicting desires and threats. 'What to do for the best?' is perhaps our most pressing question, and our deepest challenge, especially when we are living in a world that is full of opportunity, uncertainty, complexity and risk.

❝ 'What to do for the best?' is perhaps our most pressing question, and our deepest challenge, especially when we are living in a world that is full of opportunity, uncertainty, complexity and risk.❞

The research shows that we sometimes forget what really matters to us most; and sometimes act as if relatively unimportant things were actually matters of life and death. So to be really smart means to yoke our intelligent capacities to a clear and accurate sense of enlightened self-interest. Someone whose head is a noxious stew of resentments, insecurities, imagined slights and unfulfilled dreams may find it hard to know how to act 'for the best' even in relatively straightforward, everyday contexts, let alone at more obviously complex junctures. They may then act in ways that are mercurial and untrustworthy, or even apparently self-destructive. So being smart means knowing yourself, as well as being good at getting what you *think* you want.

Many surveys show that young people today are particularly prone to such pressures and confusions.[5] So education for intelligence needs to help them find and develop – in a famous and now rather tarnished phrase – their 'moral compass'. This is unlikely to happen through homilies and worksheets. They need to be helped to find what they truly love to do and want to be good at, and to see that some of the options they might consider could have toxic effects on their own deeper or longer-term well-being. They need to have the confidence to pursue and engage with all kinds of things that are difficult but worthwhile. And they need the strength of character to be able to resist courses of action that damage their own well-being, and the well-being of the social networks in which they are, like it or not, enmeshed. These things are orders of magnitude more important than whether they get a D or a C grade in their Business Studies examination when they are 16.[6] Many schools have thought hard about these deeper issues, and have their own priorities well worked out. They have developed strong cultures within which such ethical and moral issues can be raised and taken seriously by all. But not every school has.

This short journey through some of the current thinking about intelligence has thus brought us to an interesting point. The research offers suggestions about how to make schools more 'effective'; but it also challenges us to think about what 'effective' really means. An expanded and enriched concept of intelligence makes us think about the purposes of education, as well as its methods. If education is a preparation for life, and if it is to be a good preparation, regardless of how many grades a student accumulates, then that sense of purpose needs to be addressed.

> **"If education is a preparation for life, and if it is to be a good preparation, regardless of how many grades a student accumulates, then that sense of purpose needs to be addressed."**

As we say, many schools have made great progress towards helping *all* their students to become more confident and intelligent young people. But not all have, and there is more to do. Some schools even appear to side with the Professor of Worldly Wisdom in Samuel Butler's satirical book, *Erewhon*[7] when he says:

'It's not our business', he said, 'to help students to think for themselves. Surely this is the very last thing which one who wishes them well should encourage them to do. Our duty is to ensure that they shall think as we do, or at any rate, as we hold it expedient to say we do.'

We think that the research we have outlined in *New Kinds of Smart* helps to lay firm foundations for real progress in rethinking the way education can change. Supported by up-to-date information about how intelligence is learnable, schools, we hope, will feel encouraged and inspired to develop powerful, supple twenty-first-century minds in all their young people – regardless of the income bracket or the walk of life they come from, or are heading for.

Next steps

In a short book like this, all we have been able to do is offer a snapshot of some of the most obvious current directions. But, as we have said before, the territory that is opening up is both large and exciting, and there are many questions and developments that are yet to be fully explored. In this final section, we will mention just a few of the areas where our own thinking at the Centre for Real-World Learning at the University of Winchester is developing, and where we suspect there will be further progress in the next few years.

One area involves further refining the specification of the orchestra of intelligence, not just in terms of the membership, but the way the different 'instruments' are grouped. The issue is a scientific one, but it is also pragmatic: what kind of framework is most useful in helping teachers think about how they can develop their practice to capitalize on the insights emerging from the science of learnable intelligence? In our experience, three or four categories is too few, because each concept – like 'creative' or 'emotional intelligence' – is too crude to get a practical handle on. On the other hand, the 16 'habits of mind' or 17 'learning muscles' are too detailed, especially for someone new to the area, to keep tabs on. So we think a hierarchical framework, in which there are a manageable number of headings, each of which is capable of being unpacked in greater detail as the ideas become more familiar, is what is needed. Just as the orchestra has a first-level division into strings, brass, woodwind and percussion, each of which comprises a family of different instruments, so we imagine different 'sections' of the intelligent mind.

There is a second, linked, issue about how exactly to phrase the qualities of intelligence. Some of the existing frameworks are rather 'schooly', and seem still to prioritize forms of learning and problem-solving that are quite intellectual. We think, though, that the kinds of intelligence we talked about in Chapter 3 – those that involve watching, copying and practising as much as thinking and analysing – need to be fully represented within any overall model of real-world intelligence. And indeed, many schools we know do seem to be rapidly reappraising the old assumption that the 'bright' do Physics and the 'not so bright' do Plumbing and Hairdressing. So the component qualities of mind need to be phrased in a way that applies as much to 'learning by observing and practising' as 'learning by writing and arguing'.

The 4:5:1 model

We have begun work on what we call the 4:5:1 model at the Centre for Real-World Learning (see Figure 9.1). In the inner ring are what we think of as the four main compartments of the learning tool-kit: *investigating, experimenting, imagining* and *reasoning.*

Figure 9.1 The 4:5:1 model of real-world intelligence (a work in progress)

Collectively, we have borrowed Art Costa's and Bena Kallick's phrase 'habits of mind' to describe these tools. Each of these comprises a family of learnable mental habits and dispositions.

For example, *investigating* covers all the ways people go about discovering, collecting, weighing and organizing information. They read books, certainly, but they also watch things closely, copy other people, surf the internet and deliberately go looking for experience. And it is a truism, in the Google age, that being smart means being good at checking and weighing the credibility and reliability of what you find out. (It is no good teachers and parents bemoaning young people's uncritical attitude towards Wikipedia, for example, if they are still being taught in school to sit quietly and accept what they are told in science or history – much of which might actually be quite contentious or even out-of-date.) We have not talked much about how to develop 'intelligent investigating', but we think the learnability of data-gathering and careful attending is an important issue that we need to understand better.

Experimenting involves trial and error – and that means the willingness to make mistakes and to learn from them. It means being willing to tinker with things even though you don't know what is going to happen. It means being able to distinguish between an interesting, informative, energizing risk, and one where the costs of failure would be too high. It means enjoying the process of drafting and redrafting, and looking at what you have done and thinking about how you could improve it. It means knowing how to do 'good practice': how to pick out the hard parts, practise them well, and then re-embed then into the whole sonata, football game, or essay. We talked a bit about these practical forms of intelligence in Chapter 3, but there is more work to be done.

Imagining means being skilled at using the 'inner theatre' as a test-bed for learning. It means being good at 'mental rehearsal', able to use visualization as the powerful adjunct to physical practice it has been shown to be. It means knowing when and how to use reverie: as one young learner put it, 'knowing how to let your brain go soft and quiet and bubble up with ideas'. It means understanding the value (and the caveats) of intuition: knowing how to make the best use of that family of timid mental beasts called hunches, inklings, glimmerings and promptings. We discussed these forms of intelligence in Chapter 4.

And *reasoning* is the vital companion of imagination: being able to think rigorously and clearly; to follow logical chains of thought; to analyse and critique; and to assess and plan. Reasoning means exploring possible consequences, and using your experience, as well as you can, to evaluate competing ideas or courses of action. This is the traditional arena of intelligence, and nothing that we have said in this book is intended to deny its importance. But reason is one section of the mental orchestra, not the whole ensemble, and it needs to learn how to play with the instruments of investigation, experimentation and imagining, not to try to dominate them. We suspect there is a good deal to be discovered, for example, about how skilled craftsmen and virtuosi weave judicious thinking into their expertise.

The '1' in our 4:5:1 model sits in the centre, because it refers to a quality we call *presence of mind*. Presence of mind is what is required if all the instruments of intelligent learning are to be brought optimally to bear on the challenges of the present moment. It is the workspace (or the bench-top) of intelligence: the moment-to-moment engagement of the four sets of habits of mind with the whatever-it-is that is puzzling or important right now – writing the book chapter, fixing the lawnmower, amusing the baby, planning the party. This is where the intricate work of intelligent learning takes place, as tinkering leads to a new observation, which stimulates an imaginative idea, which activates a cautious train of thought, which leads to a change of tack and a new round of trial and error. Applying the right subset of your resources demands presence of mind, and we are beginning to suspect it is the key ingredient – the 'bull's eye' – of intelligence. It relates to some of the issues we discussed in Chapter 7, but we think it will involve more than merely standing back and thinking about your own thinking at key moments. We think it is a more holistic concept

191

than that, and it is one on which research is only just beginning to focus.[8]

Surrounding this engine room of intelligent learning are five attitudes or frames of mind that complement and support them. They are *curiosity, determination, resourcefulness, sociability* and *reflectiveness*. In the real world, we think it is intelligent to be inquisitive and sceptical; to be patient and resilient; to be able to make good use of the tools and resources around you; to be thoughtful and reflective; and to be capable of working, thinking and learning well with teams, families and colleagues – as well as being able to stand your ground and work on your own as well. The absence of these frames of mind leads, self-evidently, to various forms of deficiency. Lacking curiosity, you can be passive and gullible. Lacking determination you may never achieve anything worthwhile. Lacking sociability, you miss out on all the interesting and intelligent activity that goes on in groups. And lacking reflectiveness, you lack self-awareness, and the ability to see 'the big picture'. The last three of these are represented in this book. But we have had little to say about the importance of learning to be more curious, more willing to be awe-struck and better at asking darn good questions. And we have also not developed here ideas about how to develop grit and determination. A full orchestra of intelligence will need these qualities too, we think.[9]

Conversely, our 4:5:1 model does not at the moment have a place for the ethical considerations we discussed in the previous chapter – and we think it should. Perhaps we will need to expand our outer ring to include it, so the next version will be the 4:6:1 model.

We are not alone in thinking these explorations to be some of the most interesting and important that there are in science at the moment – certainly in terms of their potential implications for education. Across the world national and regional departments of education are wrestling with the composite and learnable nature of real-world intelligence and, as we have seen, some of the emergent ideas are already beginning to be reflected in the curricula of many countries, for example, New Zealand, Australia and Finland.[10] The influence of this research can be seen in the 'personal learning and thinking skills' now adopted at secondary level in England, and also in Northern Ireland's curriculum for 'thinking skills and personal capacities'.

But we are still at the beginnings of this quest to find an education that respects the treasury of the past, but uses it to build minds that are fit for an uncertain, demanding but exciting future. We hope this little book will encourage you to ask big questions about what schools are for, and how they should work; and to try out new ways of being a teacher or a school leader (or a parent or a policy-maker).

Nothing could be more important.

Notes

Prelude

1 Clark, A. (2003) *Natural Born Cyborgs: Minds, Technologies, and the Future of Human Intelligence.* Oxford: Oxford University Press.

2 Lucas, B. (ed.) (2006) *New Kinds of Smart: Emerging Thinking about What It Is to Be Intelligent Today.* London: The Talent Foundation.

3 See www.winchester.ac.uk/realworldlearning

4 For a fuller treatment of this topic, read Claxton, G. (2008) *What's the Point of School?* Oxford: Oneworld Books.

5 For a recent fuller analysis of this, see Lucas, B. and Claxton, G. (2009) Wider skills for learning; what are they, how can they be cultivated, how could they be measured and why are they important for innovation? Paper for the National Endowment for Science, Technology and the Arts, London. Available at: http://www.nesta.org.uk/wider-skills-for-learning

Chapter 1: Intelligence is Composite

1 Quoted in Mugny, G. and Carugati, F. (eds) (1989) *Social Representation of Intelligence.* Oxford: Pergamon.

2   Resnick, L. (1999) Making America smarter, *Education Week Century Series*, 18(40): 38–40.

3   Duckworth, A. and Seligman, M. (2005) Self-discipline outdoes IQ in predicting academic performance of adolescents, *Psychological Science*, 16(2): 939–44.

4   Quoted in Gould, S.J. (1995) *The Mismeasurement of Man*. New York: WW Norton, p. 149.

5   Perkins, D. (1995) *Outsmarting IQ*. New York: The Free Press.

6   Gardner, H. (1999) *Intelligence Reframed*. New York: Basic Books, p. 142.

7   See, for example, White, J. (2004) The myth of multiple intelligences, transcript of a lecture at the London Institute of Education, 17 November.

8   Gardner, H. (1984) *Frames of Mind: The Theory of Multiple Intelligence*. London: William Heinemann, p. 98.

9   Sternberg, R.J. (1996) *Successful Intelligence*. New York: Simon and Schuster.

10   Sternberg, R.J. (1997) The concept of intelligence and its role in lifelong learning and success, *American Psychologist*, 52(10): 1030–7.

11   For more about the habits of mind and various associated books, go to www.habits-of-mind.net

12   Bill subsequently replaced 'readiness' with 'responsiveness'. For a fuller treatment of his 'Rs', see Lucas, B. (2001) *Power Up Your Mind*. London: Nicholas Brealey.

13   Claxton, G. (2002) *Building Learning Power*. Bristol: TLO.

14   We acknowledge Carol Dweck at Stanford University for the creation of the helpful musculature metaphor. See Dweck, C. (2006) *Mindset*. New York: Ballantine Books.

15   Lucas, B. (ed.) (2007) *New Kinds of Smart: Emerging Thinking about What It Is to Be Intelligent Today*. London: The Talent Foundation. To find out more detail about the 16 elements described in this report, go to www.talentfoundation.com

16 To access these, go to www.habits-of-mind.net

17 We are indebted to David Perkins for the idea for this approach to 'wondering' which we have adapted from his excellent book, Perkins, D. (2009) *Making Learning Whole*. San Francisco: Jossey-Bass.

Chapter 2: Intelligence is Expandable

1 Binet, A. (1909) *Les Idées Modernes sur les Enfants*. Paris: Flammarion.

2 Blackwell, L., Trzesniewski, K. and Dweck, C. (2007) Implicit theories of intelligence predict achievement across adolescent transition: a longitudinal study and intervention, *Child Development*, 78(1): 246–63.

3 Ridley, M. (2004) *Nature via Nurture: Genes, Experience and What Makes Us Human*. London: HarperPerennial.

4 Coghlan, A. (2007) Intelligence genes keep a low profile, *New Scientist*, 1 December, pp. 272–4.

5 Dweck, C. (2006) *Mindset: The New Psychology of Success*. New York: Ballantine Books.

6 Resnick, L. (1999) Making America smarter, *Education Week Century Series*, 18(40): 38–40.

7 Bandura, A. (1997) *Self-efficacy: The Exercise of Control*. San Francisco: W.H. Freeman.

8 Rotter, J. (1972) *Applications of a Social Learning Theory of Personality*. London: Holt, Rinehart and Winston.

9 Segerstrom, S.C., Taylor, S.E., Kemeny, M.E. and Fahey, J.L. (1998) Optimism is associated with mood, coping, and immune change in response to stress, *Journal of Personality and Social Psychology*, 74(6): 1646–55.

10 Seligman, M. (1991) *Learned Optimism: How to Change Your Mind and Your Life*. New York: Alfred A. Knopf.

11 See http://www.edwdebono.com/debono/sths.htm

12 Perkins, D. (1995) *Outsmarting IQ: The Emerging Science of Learnable Intelligence*. New York: Free Press.

13 Bronson, P. (2007) How not to talk to your kids: the inverse power of praise, *New York Magazine*, 12 February.

14 Dweck, *Mindset*.

Chapter 3: Intelligence is Practical

1 Bronowski, J. (1974) *The Ascent of Man*. London: Little Brown.

2 Adapted from a story related by Robert Sternberg (1996) in *Successful Intelligence: How Practical and Creative Intelligence Determine Success in Life*. New York: Simon and Schuster.

3 Stewart, I. (1987) Are mathematicians logical?, *Nature*, 325: 386–7.

4 Ceci, S. and Liker, J. (1986) A day at the races: a study of IQ, expertise and cognitive complexity, *Journal of Experimental Psychology: General*, 115: 255–66.

5 Perkins, D. (1985) Post-primary education has little impact on informal reasoning, *Journal of Educational Psychology*, 77(5): 562–71.

6 Robinson, K. (2006) Do schools kill creativity? See http://www.ted. com/index.php/talks/ken_robinson_says_schools_kill_creativity.html

7 Ericsson, A., Krampe, R. and Tesch-Romer, C. (1993) The role of deliberate practice in the acquisition of expert performance, *Psychological Review*, 100: 363–406; also Gladwell, M. (2008) *Outliers: The Story of Success*. London: Little Brown.

8 Jorgensen, H. and Hallam, S. (2009) Practising, in S. Hallam, I. Cross and M. Thaut (eds) *The Oxford Handbook of the Psychology of Music*. Oxford: Oxford University Press. For the equivalent in sports, see, for example, Bertollo, M., Saltarelli, B. and Robazza, C. (2009) Mental preparation strategies of elite modern pentathletes, *Psychology of Sport and Exercise*, 10: 244–54; Flegal, K. and Anderson, M. (2008) Overthinking skilled motor performance: or why those who teach can't do, *Psychonomic Bulletin and Review*, 15(5): 927–32.

9 Dreyfus, H. and Dreyfus, S. (1986) *Mind over Machine*. Oxford: Wiley-Blackwell.

10 Papert, S. and Harel, I. (1991) *Constructionism*. Norwood, NJ: Ablex Publishing.

11 Andrade, J. (2009) What does doodling do?, *Applied Cognitive Psychology*, doi: 10.1002/acp.1561.

12 Goldin-Meadow, S. and Wagner, S. (2005) How our hands help us learn, *Trends in Cognitive Science*, 9(5): 234–41. Also discussed in Clark, A. (2009) *Supersizing the Mind*. Oxford: Oxford University Press.

13 Blakeslee, S. and Blakeslee, M. (2007) *The Body Has a Mind of Its Own*. New York: Random House.

14 Damasio, A. (1995) *Descartes' Error*. New York: Quill; Damasio, A. (1999) *The Feeling of What Happens*. London: Heinemann.

15 Panksepp, J. (1998) *Affective Neuroscience*. Oxford: Oxford University Press; Rolls, E.T. (1999) *The Brain and Emotion*. Oxford: Oxford University Press.

16 Prochaska, J., Norcross, J. and DiClemente, C. (1998) *Changing for Good*. New York: Avon Books; Wood, W. and Neal, D. (2007) A new look at habits and the habit-goal interface, *Psychological Review*, 114(4): 843–63.

17 For a good overview of the science and myths behind this and other potential supplements, read Centre for Educational Research and Innovation, *Understanding the Brain: the Birth of a Learning Science*, Paris: OECD, 2007.

18 For entertaining and well-informed discussions of these issues, see Goldacre, B. (2008) *Bad Science*. London: Fourth Estate, or visit http://www.badscience.net

19 See Covey, S. (1999) *Seven Habits of Highly Effective Families*. New York: Simon and Schuster.

20 See http://www.forestschools.com for more on this.

21 See http://www.ltl.org.uk

22 See http://www.tinkeringschool.com/blog/category/school-info/

23 See http://www.ted.com/index.php/talks/lang/eng/gever_tulley_on_5_ dangerous_things_for_kids.html

Chapter 4: Intelligence is Intuitive

1 Polanyi, M. (1967) *The Tacit Dimension.* London: Routledge and Kegan Paul.

2 Dijksterhuis, A. (2004) Think different: the merits of unconscious thought in preference development and decision making, *Journal of Personality and Social Psychology,* 87: 586–98; Dijksterhuis, A. and Nordgren, L. (2006) A theory of unconscious thought, *Perspectives on Psychological Science,* 1: 95–109.

3 Wilson, T. and Schooler, J. (1991) Thinking too much: introspection can reduce the quality of preferences and decisions, *Journal of Personality and Social Psychology,* 60: 181–92.

4 Google 'Women – know your limits' for an amusing illustration of this absurdity.

5 See Claxton, G. and Lucas, B. (2007) *The Creative Thinking Plan.* London: BBC Books.

6 Martindale, C. (1995) Creativity and connectionism, in S. Smith, T.B. Ward and R. Finke (eds) (1997) *The Creative Cognition Approach.* Cambridge, MA: Bradford/MIT Press.

7 Isen, A., Daubman, K. and Nowicki, G. (1987) Positive affect facilitates creative problem-solving, *Journal of Personality and Social Psychology,* 52(6): 1122–31.

8 Quoted in Fensham, P. and Marton, F. (1992) What has happened to intuition in science education?, *Research in Science Education,* 22: 114–22.

9 Ibid.

10 Einstein, A. (1973) *Ideas and Opinions.* London: Souvenir Press.

11   Bowers, K.S., Regehr, G., Balthazard, C. and Parker, K. (1990) Intuition in the context of discovery, *Cognitive Psychology*, 22: 72–110.

12   Sadler-Smith, E. (2008) *Inside Intuition*. London: Routledge.

13   Heslin, P. (2009) Better than brainstorming? Potential contextual boundary conditions to brainwriting for idea generation in organisations, *Journal of Occupational and Organizational Psychology*, 82(1): 129–45.

14   Part of this description is reprinted from Claxton, G., Edwards, L. and Scale-Constantinou, V. (2006) Cultivating creative mentalities: a framework for education, *Thinking Skills and Creativity*, 1: 57–61.

15   Gendlin, E.T. (2004) Introduction to 'Thinking at the edge', *The Folio: A Journal for Focusing and Experiential Therapy*, 19: 1–8; Larrabee, M.J. (2004) Eighth graders think at the edge, *The Folio: A Journal for Focusing and Experiential Therapy*, 19: 99–101.

16   Sternberg, R.J. (1999) The theory of successful intelligence, *Review of General Psychology*, 3: 292–316.

17   Claxton, G. and Lucas, B. (2007) *The Creative Thinking Plan*. London: BBC Books.

Chapter 5: Intelligence is Distributed

1   Pea, R. (1993) Practices of distributed intelligence and designs for education, in G. Salomon (ed.) *Distributed Cognitions: Psychological and Educational Considerations*. Cambridge: Cambridge University Press.

2   Pea, Practices.

3   This example is adapted from Clark, A. (2003) *Natural-Born Cyborgs: Minds, Technologies and the Future of Human Intelligence*. Oxford: Oxford University Press.

4   Clark, *Natural-Born Cyborgs*.

5   People's body maps, the representations of their bodies within their brains, do literally expand to incorporate new tools as part of the body.

See Blakeslee, S. and Blakeslee, M. (2007) *The Body Has a Mind of its Own*. New York: Random House.

6 See Wertsch, J. (1998) *Mind as Action*. Oxford: Oxford University Press.

7 Lodge, D. (2005) *Consciousness and the Novel*. London: Secker and Warberg; Claxton, G. (2005) *The Wayward Mind*. London: Little Brown.

8 Salomon, G. (1997) Of mind and media: how culture's symbolic forms affect learning and thinking, *Phi Delta Kappan*, 78: 375–80. See also Gee, J. (2003) *What Video Games Have to Teach Us about Learning and Literacy*. London: Palgrave Macmillan.

9 Jackson, M. (2008) *Distracted: The Erosion of Attention and the Coming Dark Age*. New York: Prometheus Books; Bauerlein, M. (2009) *The Dumbest Generation: How the Digital Age Stupefies Young Americans and Jeopardizes Our Future (Or, Don't Trust Anyone Under 30)*. Los Angeles: Jeremy P. Tarcher.

10 Salomon, G., Perkins, D., and Globerson T. (1991) Partners in cognition: extending human intelligence with intelligent technologies, *Educational Researcher*, 20(3): 2–9.

11 Salomon, G., et al., Partners.

12 von Uexkull, J. (1934) A stroll through the worlds of animals and men, in K. Lashley (ed.) *Instinctive Behaviour*. Madison, WI: International Universities Press.

13 See pages 131–2 in this book for a more detailed account of this experiment.

14 Moll, L., Tapia, J. and Whitmore, K. (1993) Living knowledge: the social distribution of cultural resources for thinking, in G. Salomon (ed.) *Distributed Cognitions*.

15 Langer, E. (1997) *The Power of Mindful Learning*. Jackson: Perseus Books.

Chapter 6: Intelligence is Social

1 Brown, P. and Lauder, H. (2000) Education, child poverty and the politics of collective intelligence, in S.J. Ball (ed.) *Sociology of Education: Major Themes*, vol. IV: *Politics and Policies*. London: RoutledgeFalmer, p. 1753.

2 Ybarra, O., Burnstein, E., Winkielman, P., Keller, M.C., Manis, M., Chan, E. and Rodriguez, J. (2008) Mental exercising through simple socializing: social interaction promotes general cognitive functioning, *Personality and Social Psychology Bulletin*, 34: 248–59.

3 In both the USA (with No Child Left Behind) and England (with Every Child Matters, http://www.everychildmatters.gov.uk/ete/personalised learning), there is a growing emphasis on personalized learning pathways.

4 Leadbeater, C. and 257 other people (2009) *We Think*. London: Profile Books.

5 Quoted in *Harpers Magazine*, 1920.

6 Vygotsky, L. (1978) *Mind and Society: The Development of Higher Mental Processes*. Cambridge, MA: Harvard University Press.

7 See, for example, Bandura, A. (1977) *Social Learning Theory*. New York: General Learning Press.

8 For a readable description of this, see Iacoboni, M., Molnar-Szakacs, I., Gallese, V., Buccino, G., Mazziotta, J. and Rizzolatti, G. (2005) Grasping the intentions of others with one's own mirror neuron system, *PLOS Biology*, 3(3): 529–35.

9 Dewey, J. (1916) *Democracy and Education*. New York: Macmillan.

10 Lave, J. and Wenger, E. (1991) *Situated Learning: Legitimate Peripheral Participation*. Cambridge: Cambridge University Press.

11 Rogoff, B. and Lave, J. (eds) (1984) *Everyday Cognition: Its Development in Social Context*. Cambridge, MA: Harvard University Press.

12 Watkins, C. (2005) Classrooms as learning communities: a review of research, *London Review of Education*, 3(1): 47–64.

13   See Wang M. et al. (1990) What influences learning: a content analysis of review literature, *Journal of Educational Research*, 84(1): 30–43.

14   Kinderman, T. (1993) Natural peer groups as contexts for individual development: the case of children's motivation in school, *Development Psychology*, 29(6): 970–7.

15   Goleman, D. (2006) *Social Intelligence: The New Science of Human Relationships*. London: Arrow Books.

16   Humphrey, N. (1984) *Consciousness Regained*. Oxford: Oxford University Press.

17   See MIT's Centre for Collective Intelligence for an overview of thinking in this area, www.cci.mit.edu

18   Hutchins, E. (1995) *Cognition in the Wild*. Cambridge, MA: MIT Press.

19   Kutnick, P. et al. (2005) Teachers' understandings of the relationship between within-class (pupil) grouping and learning in secondary schools, *Educational Research*, 47(1): 1–24.

20   Brown, A. (1997) Transforming schools into communities of thinking and learning about serious matters, *American Psychologist*, 52(4): 399–413.

21   The jigsaw technique (and variations of it which do not necessarily use the same term) have been around for nearly forty years. Its invention is often credited to distinguished psychologist Elliot Aronson (see www.jigsaw.org/history.htm). Widely used in North America it is less well known in some other parts of the world.

22   Owen, H. (2007) *Open Space Technology: A User's Guide*. San Francisco: Berrett-Koehler Publishers.

23   Lave, J. (1988) *Cognition in Practice: Mind, Mathematics and Culture in Everyday Life*. Cambridge: Cambridge University Press.

Chapter 7: Intelligence is Strategic

1   Milne, A.A. (1973) *Winnie the Pooh*. London: Heinemann Young Books.

2   German, T. and Defeyter, M. (2000) Immunity to functional fixedness in young children, *Psychonomic Bulletin and Review*, 7(4): 707–12.

3   Whitehead, A. (1911) *An Introduction to Mathematics*. Oxford: Oxford University Press.

4   Flavell, J. (1979) Metacognition and cognitive monitoring: a new area of cognitive-development inquiry, *American Psychologist*, 34: 906–11.

5   Sternberg, R. (1986) *Intelligence Applied*. New York: Harcourt Brace Jovanovich.

6   Watkins, C. (2002) *Learning about Learning Enhances Performance*. National School Improvement Network Bulletin, No. 13. London: Institute of Education.

7   See   http://www.campaign-for-learning.org.uk/cfl/learninginschools/ l2l/index.asp

8   See among many, Facer, K. and Pykett, J. (2007) *Developing and Accrediting Personal Skills and Competencies*. Bristol: FutureLab; Hoskins, B. and Fredriksson, U. (2008) *Learning to Learn: What It Is and Can It Be Measured?*, Brussels: European Commission, and http://www.oefeb.at/veranstaltung/Niemivirta_Slides.pdf?PHPSESSID= a67151d441e5bcc7fb1605eedfead565

9   See especially Schunk, D. and Zimmerman, B. (1994) *Self-regulated Learning and Performance: Issues and Educational Applications*. Hillsdale, NJ: Erlbaum.

10   Zimmerman, B. (1989) A social cognitive view of self-regulated academic learning, *Journal of Educational Psychology*, 81(3): 329–39.

11   Pintrich, P., Wolters, C. and Baxter, G. (2000) Assessing metacognition and self-regulated learning, in Schraw, G. and Ampara, J. (eds) *Issues in the Measurement of Metacognition*. Lincoln, NE: Buros Institute of Mental Measurements, University of Nebraska Press.

12   Muis, K. (2007) The role of epistemic beliefs in self-regulated learning, *Educational Psychologist*, 42(3): 173–90.

13   Schön, D. (1983) *The Reflective Practitioner: How Professionals Think in Action*. Farnham: Ashgate.

14   Perkins, D. (1995) *Outsmarting IQ: The Emerging Science of Learnable Intelligence*. New York: The Free Press.

15   Ibid, p. 113.

16   Salomon, G. and Perkins, D. (1989) Rocky roads to transfer: rethinking mechanisms of a neglected phenomenon, *Educational Psychologist*, 24(2): 113–42.

17   Perkins, D. (2009) *Making Learning Whole: How Seven Principles of Teaching Can Transform Education*. San Francisco: Jossey-Bass.

18   Philosophy for Children has become an international movement largely inspired by the work of Matthew Lipman and Gary Matthews. A quick Google search will provide a host of useful sites.

19   See http://www.qca.org.uk/qca_4336.aspx for a description of the core principles of AfL.

20   http://www.campaign-for-learning.org.uk/cfl/learninginschools/l2l/index.asp

21   See the results of research conducted by Mary James and colleagues for more about this, for example, in James, M., McCormick, R., Black, P., Carmichael, P., Drummond, M.J., Fox, A., MacBeath, J., Marshall, B., Pedder, D., Proctor, R., Swaffield, S., Swann, J. and Wiliam, D. (2007) *Improving Learning to Learn: Classrooms, Schools and Networks*. London: Routledge.

22   Leat, D. and Lin, M. (2003) Developing a pedagogy of metacognition and transfer: some signposts for the generation of knowledge and the creation of research partnerships, *British Educational Research Journal*, 29(3): 383–415.

23   For more examples, go to http://www.pz.harvard.edu/Research/ResearchVisible.htm

24   See http://www.buildinglearningpower.co.uk/blp/TrackingLearning:On-line/intro.html

Chapter 8: Intelligence is Ethical

1 Noddings, N. (1987) A morally defensible mission for schools in the 21st century, in E. Clinch (ed.) *Transforming Public Education: A New Course for America's Future*. New York: Teachers College Press, pp. 27–37.

2 Bandura, A., Ross, D. and Ross, S. (1963) Imitation of film-mediated aggressive models, *Journal of Abnormal and Social Psychology*, 66: 3–11.

3 Darley, J. and Batson, C. (1973) From Jerusalem to Jericho: a study of situational and dispositional variables in helping behaviour. *Journal of Personality and Social Psychology*, 27: 100–8.

4 Bruner, J. (1966) *Toward a Theory of Instruction*. Cambridge, MA: Harvard University Press.

5 For a telling analysis of the current situation, see Barnes, J. (2006) Meaningful schooling: researching a curriculum which makes relevance for teachers and children 5–14, paper presented at British Educational Research Association, September; Palmer, S. (2006) *Toxic Childhood: How the Modern World is Damaging Our Children and What We Can Do About It*. London: Orion Books; Claxton, G. (2008) *What's the Point of School?* Oxford: Oneworld.

6 Layard, R. and Lunn, J. (2009) *A Good Childhood*. London: Penguin Books.

7 Taken from the Youth Survey of the British Household Survey, 2006. See http://surveynet.ac.uk/sqb/qb/docs/surveys.htm

8 See, for example, the survey UNICEF (2007*) Child Poverty in Perspective: An Overview of Child Well-being in Rich Countries*. Florence: UNICEF Innocenti Research Centre.

9 Haidt, J. (2009) Obama's moral majority, *Prospect Magazine,* 155: 48–51.

10 Haidt, J. (2008) Morality, *Perspectives on Psychological Science,* 3: 65–72.

11 Handy, C. (1999) *The Hungry Spirit: Beyond Capitalism – a Quest for Purpose in the Modern World.* New York: Broadway Books.

12 For a more detailed description of these stages of moral development, see Kohlberg, L. (1984) *Essays on Moral Development,* vol. II: *The Psychology of Moral Development.* San Francisco: Harper and Row.

13 Peterson, C. and Seligman, M. (2004) *Character Strengths and Virtues: A Handbook and Classification.* Oxford: Oxford University Press and American Psychological Association.

14 Claxton, G. (2008) Wisdom; advanced creativity? In A. Craft., H. Gardner and G. Claxton (eds) *Creativity, Wisdom and Trusteeship: Exploring the Role of Education.* Thousand Oaks, CA: Corwin Press.

15 See Claxton *What's the Point of School?*

16 Gardner, G. (2006) *Five Minds for the Future.* Boston, MA: Harvard Business School Press.

17 Noddings, N. (1999) Two concepts of caring, in *Philosophy of Education Society Yearbook,* see http://www.ed.uiuc.edu/EPS/PES-yearbook/1999/noddings.asp

18 Crick, B. (1998) *Education for Citizenship and the Teaching of Democracy in Schools* (The Crick Report). London: HMSO.

19 To download this, go to http://www.character.org/uploads/PDFs/Pub_Quality_Standards_.pdf

20 Scales, P., Blyth, D., Berkas, T. and Kielsmeier, J. (2000) The effects of service-learning on middle school students' social responsibility and academic success, *Journal of Early Adolescence,* 20(3): 332–58.

21 Quoted in Lovat, T. and Clement, N. (2008) The pedagogical imperative of values education, *Journal of Beliefs and Values,* 29(3): 273–85.

Chapter 9: Finale

1 Resnick, L. (1999) Making America smarter, *Education Week Century Series,* 18(40): 38–40.

2   Piaget, J. (2001) *The Psychology of Intelligence*. London: Routledge.

3   See www.habits-of-mind.net

4   Claxton, G. (2002) *Building Learning Power*. Bristol: TLO.

5   See, for example, the recent Children's Society Report by Richard Layard and Judy Dunn (2009) *A Good Childhood: Searching for Values in a Competitive Age*. Harmondsworth: Penguin Books.

6   These are the high-stakes examinations that are called GCSEs in the UK.

7   For a contemporary reprint of this book, see Butler, S. (2006) *Erewhon*. London: Penguin Classics.

8   See Senge, P., Scharmer, C., Jaworski, J. and Flowers, B. (2005) *Presence*. London: Nicholas Brealey.

9   For a detailed exploration of the idea of 'grit', see Roberts, Y. (2009) *Grit: The Skills for Success and How They Are Grown*. London: The Young Foundation.

10 For a fuller description and analysis of these frameworks, see Lucas, B. and Claxton, G. (2009) *Wider Skills for Learning: What Are They, How Can They Be Cultivated, How Could They Be Measured and Why Are They Important for Innovation?* London: National Endowment for Science, Technology and the Arts.

Select Bibliography

Clark, A. (2003) *Natural Born Cyborgs: Minds, Technologies, and the Future of Human Intelligence*. Oxford: Oxford University Press.

Claxton, G. (2002) *Building Learning Power*. Bristol: TLO.

Claxton, G. (2008) *What's the Point of School?* Oxford: Oneworld Books.

Craft, A., Gardner H. and Claxton, G. (2008) *Creativity, Wisdom and Trusteeship: Exploring the Role of Education*. Thousand Oaks, CA: Corwin Press.

Dweck, C. (2006) *Mindset: The New Psychology of Success.* New York: Ballantine Books.

Gardner, H. (2006) *Five Minds for the Future.* Boston, MA: Harvard Business School Press.

Hattie, J. (2009) *Visible Learning: A Synthesis of Over 800 Meta-analyses Relating to Achievement.* London: Routledge.

Langer, E. (1997) *The Power of Mindful Learning.* Jackson: Perseus Books.

Lave, J. and Wenger, E. (1991) *Situated Learning: Legitimate Peripheral Participation.* Cambridge: Cambridge University Press.

Lucas, B. (2001) *Power Up Your Mind.* London: Nicholas Brealey.

Lucas, B. (ed.) (2006) *New Kinds of Smart: Emerging Thinking about What It Is to Be Intelligent Today.* London: The Talent Foundation.

Perkins, D. (1995) *Outsmarting IQ*. New York: The Free Press.

Perkins, D. (2009) *Making Learning Whole*. San Francisco: Jossey-Bass.

Peterson, C. and Seligman, M. (2004) *Character Strengths and Virtues: A Handbook and Classification*. Oxford: Oxford University Press and American Psychological Association.

Resnick, L. (1999) Making America smarter, *Education Week Century Series*, 18(40): 38–40.

Rogoff, B. and Lave, J. (eds) (1984) *Everyday Cognition: Its Development in Social Context*. Cambridge MA: Harvard University Press.

Sternberg, R. (1996) *Successful Intelligence*. New York: Simon & Schuster.

Watkins, C. (2002) Learning about learning enhances performance. *National School Improvement Network Bulletin*, No. 13. London: Institute of Education.

Index

211